Happily
MARRIED
FOR
Life

Happily

MARRIED
FOR

Life

60 TIPS FOR A FUN
GROWING RELATIONSHIP

LARRY J. KOENIG, PH.D.

LIFE JOURNEY®

Bringing Home the Message for Life

COOK COMMUNICATIONS MINISTRIES
Colorado Springs, Colorado • Paris, Ontario
KINGSWAY COMMUNICATIONS LTD
Eastbourne, England

Life Journey® is an imprint of
Cook Communications Ministries, Colorado Springs, CO 80918
Cook Communications, Paris, Ontario
Kingsway Communications, Eastbourne, England

HAPPILY MARRIED FOR LIFE
© 2006 by Larry J. Koenig, PhD

The Web addresses (URLs) recommended throughout this book are
solely offered as a resource to the reader. The citation of these Web
sites does not in any way imply an endorsement on the part of the
author or the publisher, nor does the author or publisher vouch for
their content for the life of this book.

Published in association with the literary agency of Mark Gilroy
Communications, 6528 E 101st St., Ste. 416, Tulsa, OK 74133-6754.

Cover Design: Disciple Design
Cover Photo Credit: © BigStock Photo

First Printing, 2006
Printed in the United States of America

1 2 3 4 5 6 7 8 9 10 Printing/Year 11 10 09 08 07 06

All scripture quotations, unless otherwise noted, are taken from the
Holy Bible, New International Version®. *NIV*®. Copyright © 1973, 1978,
1984 by International Bible Society. Used by permission of
Zondervan. All rights reserved.

ISBN-13: 978-0-7814-4307-4
ISBN-10: 0-7814-4307-5

LCCN: 2006920259

To my Beloved
Nydia

ACKNOWLEDGMENTS

While writing a book, your life can get a little crazy. It takes a lot of time and concentration—two things you have to borrow away from other parts of your life if you want to get the task done. This borrowing of time and attention from your family only works if you have a willing mate, one that is amenable to be awakened at 4:30 every morning as you slip out of bed to write, and one willing to listen to endless ideas and theories about marriage. So, first and foremost, I must acknowledge my beloved wife, Nydia. She is truly my all in all, the wind beneath my wings. Without our deep love and daily devotion to one another, this book would be but a sham. Thank you, Nydia.

Current research points out that if you want to predict how a man will treat his wife you can do so by observing how his father treats his mother. How fortunate I have been to have had my father to show me how to treat a woman in such a way that love would grow day after day, year after year, into a deeply satisfying and happy marriage. All who knew my father knew that he loved my mother with all of his heart. It was in his every action and part of his very being. He exuded love for my mother. It has always been my dream to have a marriage like that of my parents and because of them I now do. Thank you, Dad.

Besides also being a powerful and positive role model of how to love and be happily married, my mother deserves a bit more appreciation. It is her continued support and encouragement that has helped keep me writing over the years. It is from her, too, that I inherited a love of reading and a gift for writing. If I keep writing I hope one day to write as well as she does. Thank you, Mother.

For quite a few years now I have been blessed with the friendship of Dr. Tony and Susan Ioppolo. They, too, have the kind of love that is deep and obvious to all those around them. Their encouragement, insights, and friendship over the years have made more of a difference in my life than they can imagine. Thank you, Tony and Susan.

Then there is my dear friend and fellow author Max Davis. Besides being one of the best friends a person could have, Max has suggested the right agents to get my books published, helped me prepare book proposals correctly, role modeled how to be a published author, and encouraged me to keep going when all seemed hopeless. Thank you, Max.

Anyone looking at this book can see what a wonderful job Cook Communications Ministries did in designing and producing it. To all of you at Cook, thank you.

To the many others who have helped me along the way, I only hope you know that I love you all and appreciate your efforts on my behalf from the depths of my heart. Thank you all.

CONTENTS

INTRODUCTION

The difference between having a joy-filled marriage and a miserable one filled with strife is enormous. Yet spouses are expected to figure out how to be successfully married with very little instruction. How absurd!

Can you imagine building a house without knowing how? The result would likely be an unstable house with a leaky roof. Chances are, it would fall down on your head sooner or later.

The same applies to marriages. A good marriage doesn't just build itself. If you want a joy-filled, lasting marriage, then it's a really good idea to get some instruction on how to achieve one. This book gives clear, concise guidelines on how to build your marriage into a relationship filled with joy and satisfaction.

Can you remember the honeymoon stage of your marriage? Life was bliss; you felt like the luckiest person in the world. And you were blessed with the certainty that you and your spouse would have the best marriage on earth. When you heard the words "marriage is difficult," you didn't relate; you likely even felt sorry that everyone didn't have the trouble-free relationship you and your spouse did.

Research shows that the honeymoon phase typically lasts about two years. However, many couples will tell you their honeymoon ended before they got home from the trip.

Perhaps you are still in the honeymoon phase. If so, enjoy every minute of it. This delightful time in a couple's relationship is short—or so they say.

But why? Why can't marital bliss last forever? For much of my professional life I believed, like most, that it's unrealistic to think couples could stay blissfully married. I now know different. I have come to realize that couples can stay married and remain wonderfully happy with each other.

I have such a marriage with my wife, Nydia. We're among the many couples that get minimal press. Little is reported on the couples that are enormously happy in their marriages. The focus in the media is on the negative, on the marriages that end in misery and divorce. The focus of *Happily Married for Life* is on how to stay wonderfully and happily married. Any time you see the words, "how to," it implies three things. First, that it's possible to do something. Second, there's a process for doing so. Third, others have successfully followed the process and achieved the desired result.

You can expect the same from *Happily Married for Life*. By reading and implementing the ideas in this book, you can and will improve your marriage. At the same time, both you and your spouse will come to deepen your love for one another. That's my promise to you. And, that's my prayer for you, too!

Chapter 1

How to Use This Book

The primary purpose of *Happily Married for Life* is to help people build and maintain happy and enduring marriages. The book does this in two ways: 1) by teaching couples how to avoid conflicts or keep them from escalating and 2) by helping them choose behaviors, strategies, and solutions that will then satisfy their needs and those of their partners.

Throughout the book you will find strategies to help you avoid or successfully resolve conflicts, as well as ideas for enhancing different areas of your relationship. All the suggestions offered here are designed to help couples choose to say and do the things that result in marital harmony.

When reading the book, try strategies that seem to fit your personality and relationship. If one doesn't seem comfortable to you, go on to one that does. You'll find that the ideas that appeal to you aren't necessarily ones that appeal to others, and vice versa; people vary. So, at least in the beginning, I suggest couples stick to the strategies that feel most comfortable. Later, you may want to risk a little and try some of the ideas that didn't immediately appeal to you. In doing so, you may find some suggestions that are surprisingly useful.

This is an experiential book. Most chapters end with what I call "love potions," which are designed to help you get all the love you want from your marriage. Practicing these "potions" should grow and strengthen the bond between you—and many of them are a lot of fun. The more you practice the love potions, the more you'll get out of them.

Although the chapters build on preceding chapters, readers can nonetheless skip around. A number of chapters start with some of the most up-to-date information available on marriage. Some chapters consist strictly of questions. These are designed to help you get to know your partner better, which will also strengthen the bond between you. As an added bonus, they give you great practice in communicating with each other.

Ready? Just pick a place and dive into the book. It is my hope that your marriage will come out dripping with great ways to enliven your relationship!

Chapter 2

PRINCIPLES OF HARMONY: PART 1

J oy-filled marriages depend on the needs of each partner being met. This is essential. If needs are met, love thrives. If they are not, love dies. Also, the more often needs are met for each person in the marriage, the higher the level of satisfaction and joy. So, the question is, how can couples get their needs met on a continual basis?

The answer may shock you. You may reject it outright. But, as I lay out the evidence, you will see that there's no other realistic way for marriages to thrive. Here is the key to getting your marital needs fulfilled: *You must take responsibility for identifying and satisfying your spouse's needs.*

Now go back, and reread that last sentence a couple of times. If you are like many people, part of you is clamoring, "Hey, what about *my* needs?" Good question. And here's the answer. The more you identify and satisfy your spouse's needs, the more willing and able your spouse will be to identify and satisfy your needs.

You will find proof in this book that this is true. And you will also find delightful ways to identify and satisfy the needs of your spouse. By doing so, your own needs will get met and the joy in your marriage will soar!

PRINCIPLE NO. 1: YOU AND YOUR SPOUSE HAVE NEEDS

My wife, Nydia (rhymes with Lydia), loves African violets. You should see them. She has fourteen plants in a window seat in our kitchen. Besides the natural light from the windows, she has spotlights above fitted with grow lights. On a regular schedule she waters these plants and keeps them fertilized. Of course, she also talks to them in a loving, nurturing tone. To keep up on the latest ideas for caring for African violets, she subscribes to a magazine dedicated to their care and propagation.

The result is beautiful African violets. Their leaves are huge and healthy. They bloom with astonishingly beautiful flowers for months at a time. They are a delight to the eyes.

If you are like me, you know what it's like to ignore a plant's needs. We know what happens if we leave a plant unattended. Without water and fertilizer, it withers and eventually dies, brown and irrevocably dead! At this point there's little left to do but to throw the plant out and soothe our guilt feelings by promising never to ignore a plant again.

Your marriage is like a plant. In fact, your spouse is like a plant. He or she has needs. If your marriage is to thrive, then you must help your spouse attend to these needs. The happiness and endurance of your marriage depends on how well you do so.

PRINCIPLE NO. 2: SMALL ACTS OF KINDNESS FERTILIZE MARRIAGES

The prevailing attitude in professional circles is that everyone is responsible for their own needs. For a long time I thought so, too. But then I started to notice that the couples whose marriages are happiest attend to each other's needs as well as their own. In fact, they very often put the needs of their spouse over their own. Hmmm. Now that's interesting.

If you look at long-lasting, happy marriages, what you find is that each spouse is attuned to the other's needs. They anticipate and fulfill them without the other even asking.

Things like this happen: A husband stops at the store on the way home from work to buy pop; not because he drinks it but because he noticed there wasn't any more in the fridge for his wife, who loves it. The wife, on another occasion, reminds her husband when he's busy doing something else that his favorite TV program is about to start.

The examples could go on and on. What I've come to notice about these couples is that the things they do for one another are typically small, seemingly insignificant things. And their days are filled with such activities. These small acts of kindness are the same to a marriage as the light, watering, and fertilizer are to a plant (of course, gentle, encouraging words spoken daily in a marriage help a lot, too!). What they add up to is an environment that helps create a couple that is happily married for a lifetime.

PRINCIPLE NO. 3: A DUAL FOCUS PRODUCES HARMONY

When people first fall in love and begin to court, they bend over backward to please each other. To be sure, they watch out for their own needs, but they focus on satisfying the needs of their lover as well. At times, each will even let the fulfillment of the other person's needs take precedence over his own needs. But, even in the early stages of love, harmony requires the couple to focus on the needs of both of them. And with harmony, love grows.

For harmony—and thus love—to continue to grow, both people must remain aware of and continue to act to satisfy their own needs as well as the needs of their partner.

Marriages stay healthy when both people have their needs met. In the best marriages, partners take responsibility for their own needs. And they take responsibility for being aware of their spouse's needs and for helping to meet them. The more this happens, the happier a marriage becomes.

PRINCIPLES OF HARMONY: PART 2

PRINCIPLE NO. 4: A SINGULAR FOCUS PRODUCES DISCORD

In marriage, when one partner is focused only on satisfying her own needs, discord is likely. This is often true in the short term and almost always true in the long term.

When it comes down to it, people will not cooperate with their spouses if their own needs aren't being met. They may do so in given short-term situations, but over the long haul they'll refuse to do so. Instead, feeling that their needs aren't being met, they will withdraw emotionally—and often legally—from the marriage.

PRINCIPLE NO. 5: HARMONY IS A CHOICE

Even in the early stages of a relationship, harmony results from lovers choosing to do things that will satisfy themselves as well as their partners. But it doesn't take much effort to do so because of their romantic feelings. A large part of romantic love is made up of an acute desire to cater to the needs of the person who is at the same time catering to your own needs.

As people progress in their marriages, it gets tougher. Expectations for need fulfillment don't get met, and attitudes change from a confidence that the lack of fulfillment is an exception to the happy relationship to a conviction the spouse is being unfeeling and selfish in not meeting the partner's needs. People become angry, hurt, and resentful. When this happens, the injured person typically stops meeting his spouse's expectations as well.

To stop this cycle from destroying the marriage, choices must be consciously made to focus on each other's needs and proactive plans for harmony executed. Then each person must take responsibility for satisfying some of his own needs while also taking into account the needs of his spouse.

It's a fantasy to think harmony will exist in a marriage without this kind of attention. It will not. Like plants, if you ignore the needs of your spouse, your love will die as assuredly as will a plant left unwatered. Discord will result instead. Relationships erode over time when needs go unmet. For a marriage to flourish it's absolutely essential that the partners be proactive in becoming aware of and attending to their partner's needs as well as their own.

PRINCIPLE NO. 6: YOU CAN HEAL A MARRIAGE

You can heal a marriage by focusing on and satisfying your spouse's needs. But, you have to be patient. It takes time— sometimes lots of time.

Here's the thing to remember. Love never fails! The apostle Paul tells us that in 1 Corinthians 13, and we all had his words on love read at our weddings. What it means is that if you lovingly attend to your spouse's needs, even if he or she is unable or unwilling to meet yours at the time, your love will one day be returned. When it does, it will flourish.

This takes patience. Especially when your efforts at showing love aren't returned or, worse yet, are rebuffed. I think it helps to know, though, that everyone of us goes through periods in our life of great stress. While I don't want to condone self-centered behavior, I want to recognize that some periods of stress and personal challenge cripple a person's ability to focus on anyone's needs but their own.

Unfortunately, these times can be extended. Where the real danger comes is if the other spouse gets fed up with not having his needs met. If this happens, watch out. Conflicts escalate, and people often seek solace outside of their marriages. Both can ruin the marriage.

As difficult as it is, if you can persevere and focus on satisfying your spouse's needs without expectation of your love being returned, your marriage will likely survive and ultimately thrive.

If you ever need to heal your marriage without much or any help from your spouse, use the **Marital Law of Reciprocity.** This law states that however you consistently treat your spouse is how your spouse will ultimately treat you. If you treat your spouse with love and compassion, he or she will eventually treat you with love and compassion. Of course, this is a double-edged sword as the negative applies as well.

This law applies over time and very consistently produces results. There are some guidelines to its effective use, though. You must have faith that your spouse will respond positively, yet you must *not* expect or demand that your spouse respond positively by a given time. If you expect him or her to respond in kind or on the spot, you set yourself up for disappointment and, worse yet, resentment.

This law also works best if you keep acting in love even if you see no results whatsoever. Tough to do? Certainly! Especially if your spouse responds negatively. But the payoff will be a lasting, love-filled marriage.

Chapter 4

What Is Your Love Dialect?

Dr. Gary Chapman, in his marriage program and book *The Five Love Languages*, points out that each person in a marriage has a favorite way of giving and receiving love. I agree. In fact, there are five distinct behaviors people engage in to communicate their love: actions, attentive togetherness, physical expressions, positive strokes, and gift-giving.

The idea of "love dialects" is based on several premises:

1. People give love the way they like to receive love.
2. Partners rarely have the same predominant way of giving and receiving love.
3. When our partner expresses love the way we like— our "love dialect"—we feel loved.
4. When our partner expresses love to us in a different "love dialect," the effort often goes unnoticed.

Simply put, if you don't express your love in a form your spouse understands, he or she will likely fail to interpret the expression as love.

Knowing your own love dialect will make it easier to communicate the types of actions that make you feel loved, and getting to know your spouse's dialect will help you plan the kinds of things that will make him or her feel loved. Following is a test you can take to determine your own love dialect. This can serve two purposes: First, it will tell you the ways you prefer to give and receive love; and second, it will give your spouse concrete ideas for making you feel loved.

Instructions: Rate each of the following statements according to how strongly you feel it represents the way you give and receive love. Try not to share your answers until both of you have finished. Use the following scale:

"1" if the statement is rarely true about the way you give and receive love

"2" if the statement is sometimes true about you

"3" if the statement is often true about you

"4" if the statement is an excellent representation of how you give and receive love

____ 1. I feel loved when you do something I ask.

____ 2. I feel loved when you maintain eye contact with me while I am talking.

____ 3. I love it when you ask me for a hug.

____ 4. When you compliment me I feel especially loved.

____ 5. I love it when you bring me gifts.

____ 6. When you jump in to help me do things, I really appreciate it.

____ 7. I need to spend some time really talking with you every day.

____ 8. I wish you would kiss me more often.

____ 9. I think about your compliments long after you give them.

____ 10. When you surprise me with little gifts, I sense how much you care.

____ 11. I often comment to other people about how much you help me get things done.

____ 12. It doesn't really matter what we're doing; I just enjoy being with you.

____ 13. I could enter "the longest kissing contest" with you and enjoy every minute.

____ 14. When you say nice things about me, it's music to my ears.

____ 15. What I look forward to more than anything is giving and receiving gifts.

____ 16. When I want to express my love, I first think of what I might do special for you.

____ 17. I think the best way to spell love is T-I-M-E.

____ 18. I wish we would hug and cuddle more often.

____ 19. More than anything, I think it's important to say "I love you" at least once a day.

____ 20. I spend a lot of time picking out gifts. After all, the perfect gift is a great way to say "I love you."

____ 21. The more things you do for me, the more I feel loved.

____ 22. More than anything, I look forward to the time we spend together.

____ 23. To tell you the truth, the way to my heart is through physical expressions of love.

____ 24. I absolutely love writing and receiving love notes.

____ 25. If I were rich, I would buy you a gift every day.

____ 26. I constantly look for ways to do things for you. That's how I express my love best.

____ 27. You can tell how much I love you just by how much time I spend doing things with you.

____ 28. If you want to show me how much you love me, then you will be wonderfully affectionate.

____ 29. You can count on me to give you lots of appreciation and praise.

____ 30. Whenever I'm feeling especially loving, I start looking for a gift to give you.

LOVE DIALECT SCORING SHEET

Now go back and add 3 to the statements you feel most accurately describe the way you give and receive love. Then transfer your answers to the corresponding blanks on the following page. You will find this an easy task if you go across the rows of blanks instead of down. Be sure to add in the points for the statements you felt most strongly represent the way you give and receive love.

After you transfer your answers, add the columns up and record the total at the bottom. The highest score will represent the way in which you best like to give and receive love.

Actions	Attentive Togetherness	Physical Expressions
1. _____	2. _____	3. _____
6. _____	7. _____	8. _____
11. _____	12. _____	13. _____
16. _____	17. _____	18. _____
21. _____	22. _____	23. _____
26. _____	27. _____	28. _____
Totals:	Totals:	Totals:
_____	_____	_____

Positive Strokes	Gift Giving
4. _____	5. _____
9. _____	10. _____
14. _____	15. _____
19. _____	20. _____
24. _____	25. _____
29. _____	30. _____
Totals:	Totals:
_____	_____

Chapter 5

How to Speak Your Spouse's Love Dialect

Now that you know your spouse's dialect, you'll want to put this information to use. The more ways you express your love according to your spouse's love dialect, the more your spouse will feel loved. And the more loved your spouse feels, the more he or she will want to reciprocate.

Following are the five love dialects and suggested types of loving behaviors for each. Talk them over with your spouse, put a check by the ones that appeal to you most and add other suggestions in the blanks provided.

ACTIONS

If your mate's primary love dialect is through actions, you'll want to express your love through:
1. babysitting
2. household maintenance
3. special projects
4. yard work
5. remodeling
6. doing the dishes
7. helping children with homework
8. doing laundry

9. helping with elderly parents
10. grocery shopping
11. nursing through an illness
12. _____
13. _____
14. _____
15. _____

ATTENTIVE TOGETHERNESS

If your spouse's love dialect is attentive togetherness, you'll want to express your love through:

1. sitting and talking
2. going out for a romantic dinner
3. going for long walks together
4. going on picnics
5. going shopping together
6. going antique hunting together
7. taking up a sport together
8. taking up a hobby together
9. reading out loud to one another
10. worshipping together
11. attending sporting events together
12. _____
13. _____
14. _____
15. _____

Physical Expressions

If your spouse's love dialect is physical expressions, you will want to express your love through:

1. hugs
2. kissing
3. making love (with lots of foreplay)
4. holding hands
5. blowing kisses
6. wrestling
7. tickling
8. making goo-goo eyes
9. massages
10. cuddling
11. spooning
12. _____
13. _____
14. _____
15. _____

Positive Strokes

If your spouse's love dialect is positive strokes, you'll want to express your love through:

1. love notes strategically hidden to be found throughout the day
2. complimenting clothes
3. complimenting hair
4. complimenting physical attributes
5. expressing gratitude for doing ordinary things like house or yard work
6. expressing appreciation for listening and understanding

7. expressing appreciation for taking care of children or working
8. saying "I love you" morning, noon, and night
9. buying special greeting cards
10. writing poetry expressing your love
11. writing love letters
12. _____
13. _____
14. _____
15. _____

Receiving Gifts

If your spouse's love dialect is receiving gifts, you'll want to express your love through:

1. giving small surprise gifts
2. sending flowers
3. buying candy
4. shopping together at the mall
5. buying birthday presents
6. buying lots of Christmas presents
7. wrapping gifts beautifully
8. making opening gifts a special event and/or big production
9. taking pictures of the gift-opening event
10. giving gifts for no particular reason
11. hiding gifts under his or her pillow
12. _____
13. _____
14. _____
15. _____

Love Potion

Surprise your spouse at least once a week for the next month with some expression of love that fits his or her love dialect. Make it something as special as possible. Also, remember to express appreciation when your spouse expresses love to you in your love dialect.

Chapter 6

THE MOST COMMON METHOD OF MOTIVATING CHANGE IN A MARRIAGE

During the honeymoon phase, lovers are mostly blind to each other's faults. In short, they see their partner as "perfect." When asked if there's anything they would change about each other, the answer is normally a loving, "No, Sweetheart. Don't change a thing. I love you just the way you are."

Of course, once the "honeymoon" is over, it's another story. The blinders come off and the flaws are revealed. What a shock this can be! For some, it can be like parking a shiny brand new car out in the grocery store parking lot and coming out to find it all dented up. For others, it's a slower process in which the awareness of flaws dawns on them over a period of years. But the result is the same. What was once flawless is now viewed as damaged goods.

In some respects, it's worse than this. We tend to view faults as being under the conscious control of our partner. At first they're pointed out with great care and kindness with a request for change, something like: "Darling, I love you so much. Can I tell you something without you getting mad? I can? Well, I know it's a small thing and I don't want to nitpick, but would you mind keeping your dirty socks off the kitchen table?"

No matter what the immediate response, be it positive or negative, the person tends not to change. Habits, we all know, are extremely difficult to break. So, in the given scenario, the offender absentmindedly goes right back to leaving his socks on the kitchen table. Now the couple is on a track to conflict.

Repeated offenses are now met with criticism—the most common method of motivating change in a marriage. Criticism is based on two assumptions. The first is that our partner is oblivious to his faults and therefore needs them to be pointed out. The second assumption is that the criticism needs to be harsh in order to motivate the person to change.

Based on these assumptions, the complaining partner, angry now that her request for change is being ignored, ends up saying something like, "Do you know what your problem is? No? Then let me tell you. You are the messiest person I've ever met. And you have no regard for my needs whatsoever. I'm tired of always having to pick up after you. If you really loved me, you would change!"

Insight plus motivation. This would seem to be a good thing. But it isn't. The problem is that criticism destroys relationships because of our nature as human beings.

Human beings will not remain in a positive relationship with someone who is always critical. We simply will not do it. Instead, we'll do one of two things: Either we'll get away from the person or, if we feel trapped, we'll try to make that person as miserable as he is making us.

Couples cannot afford to get into a cycle of criticizing each other. Millions of couples have lousy relationships, and many of them got that way through well-intended criticism. The good news is that there are also millions of couples who have wonderful, happy relationships. But they've learned to handle their spouses' faults much differently.

The next chapter looks at some of the other maladaptive ways people in marriages deal with conflict. The chapter after that discusses the positive ways successful couples handle faults.

Love Potion

Go to a movie. After the movie, go somewhere for a snack and pick out two couples each to discuss — one couple you know whose relationship you admire and another whose marriage you think is headed for the divorce courts. Discuss why you think each couple has a great or a lousy marriage.

Add to this discussion your views on criticism. Answer the question, "Is constructive criticism okay?" If so, "What is the difference between constructive and destructive criticism?"

Chapter 7

DYSFUNCTIONAL STRATEGIES FOR RESOLVING DIFFERENCES

Most of us learned how to get what we wanted by watching and copying our parents' behavior. Though intellectually we may recognize what was good and what was bad in the way our parents resolved conflicts, we end up repeating the maladaptive behaviors anyway. Other dysfunctional methods of conflict resolution come about simply for lack of positive role models to learn from. Fear of dealing with the possible wrath that might be born out of confronting a negative situation can also cause a person to adopt ineffective conflict resolution measures.

There are so many negative ways to respond to conflict that it's no wonder couples have so much trouble solving problems.

This is why couples often try to get what they want by employing one of the following strategies:

1. Anger
2. Defensiveness, making excuses
3. Withdrawing physically
4. Revenge
5. Sarcasm
6. Contempt
7. Put-downs
8. Guilt trips
9. Violence

10. Placating
11. Stonewalling
12. Cross-complaining
13. Yes/but-ing
14. Whining
15. Broken record syndrome
16. Denying responsibility
17. Blaming
18. Drinking
19. Taking drugs
20. Throwing in the kitchen sink
21. Making threats
22. Escaping (all kinds: television, books, computers, friends, sleep, food, etc.)
23. "Rubber Man/Rubber Woman" syndrome
24. Lying
25. Sulking
26. "Poor Me" syndrome
27. Pushing buttons
28. Complaining incessantly
29. Refusing to cooperate
30. Throwing a temper tantrum

Two of these strategies may need explanation. Throwing in the kitchen sink is when an argument starts and one or both participants bring up every wrong thing the other person did that they can think of, both past and present. The "Rubber Man/Rubber Woman" syndrome is when one person has a complaint and the other simply bounces the same complaint back. For example: "You never listen to me!" followed by "Well, you never listen to me either!"

None of the above takes any practice. All of us have dealt with our conflicts in one or several of these dysfunctional ways. One of the worst things we can do is reinforce the use of these strategies by giving in to someone who employs them. If they are effective, they will be used over and over until the marriage breaks irretrievably.

Clearly, the ability to resolve conflicts is a prerequisite for a happy and stable marriage. It's also one of the most difficult tasks of the marital relationship. It takes a lot of effort, but couples who wish to live happily together will find healthy ways to resolve conflict and adaptive ways of negotiating for what they want.

Love Potion #3

Individually go over the list and admit to your-self which of the dysfunctional strategies you employ to get your way or resolve conflicts. Pledge that you won't use these methods for the next week. Resolve instead to use some of the strategies described in upcoming chapters. Now, go surprise your spouse with something nice. Or, surprise your spouse by doing something nice.

Chapter 8

THE EASIEST WAY TO RESOLVE CONFLICT

As I said previously, being able to successfully deal with and resolve conflict is a prerequisite for a long and happy marriage. In the last chapter I talked about the kinds of dysfunctional strategies people try to use to settle conflicts. Now, I'll offer the first of several healthy ways you can resolve conflict so you can get more of what you want out of your marriage.

Resolving conflict and getting what you want are very much the same tasks. Conflict results from dissatisfaction; dissatisfaction comes about because we aren't getting what we want. Therefore, resolving conflict becomes a process of learning how to get what we want. Of course, in a marriage we want to do this in a way that preserves the love between us and our spouses.

The easiest and most functional way of getting what you want in your relationship is a two-step process. First, you need to decide what you want. While this sounds easy, it may take some reflection. We tend to know what we want, but we aren't always good at defining it in a way that we can communicate to another person. So, the first thing to do is to take a pad and pencil and write down what you want. If at first you find what you've written to be unclear or unsatisfying, keep writing until you are satisfied with it.

Once you are clear on what you want, ask your spouse for it. Don't justify it in any way; simply ask for what you want. But do make sure to ask with a positive attitude and a positive expectation that you will get it.

Requests can be simple or complex. For instance:

1. Would you please help me fold the laundry?
2. Would you please help me paint the fence?
3. Would you please watch the kids on Thursday nights so I can take a karate class?
4. Would you please go out to dinner and a movie with me on Friday night?
5. Would you please go to the doctor and take care of your snoring problem?
6. Would you please pick up your socks?
7. Would you mind if I went fishing with my friends on Saturday?
8. Can we set a time when we can talk over some issues that have been bothering me?
9. Would you please have sex with me tonight?
10. Would you please take me out on Saturday evening?

Simple requests can work wonders. It's important to remember to only make the request. Leave off the reasons why. Just make the direct request.

For many people, making simple requests is difficult. However, simple, clear requests are the easiest way to get what you want. They're also the most functional way of resolving conflicts. Often, rather than get into a big fight over how your spouse never does what you want, you can avoid the fight altogether by simply asking for what you want. If you can do this and not fire any shots at your spouse in the process, you are much more likely to get what you want while avoiding a conflict.

Some people object to this process because they have one of two negative attitudes about asking. One of these goes like this: "Why should I have to ask? My spouse knows what needs to be done and he should just do it without my having to ask." Another attitude goes like this: "Why should I have to ask my spouse for anything? I'm an adult now and I should be able to do whatever I want without having to ask."

The answer to both of these objections is the same. If you ask for what you want, you will get more of what you want, you will avoid conflict, and you will likely preserve your marriage.

Of course, it's possible your spouse will say no. But you'll get more of what you want if you ask with the attitude that your spouse has every right to say no. If your spouse does say no, say something like, "I respect your right to say no and I'll bet you have some good reasons for saying no. Would you tell me what they are?"

Sometimes if you respond non-defensively when someone says no, he'll change his mind almost immediately. I think this is because often we're programmed to say no automatically even when we have little or no reason to do so.

If this doesn't get you what you want and you are still determined to achieve your goal, try some of the other strategies presented in upcoming chapters.

Love Potion

Make a list of some things you want your spouse to do. Pick four things from the list and ask for one of them each week for a month.

If you find you have trouble asking for what you want, read Mark Victor Hansen and Jack Canfield's book, *The Aladdin Factor.* It's a wonderful book about how to ask for and get what you want. This is also a great book to read if you want more success in your career. Now go ask your spouse for a bear hug.

Chapter 9

THE KEY TO SOLVING ALL MARITAL CONFLICT

The key to solving all marital conflict is to identify and satisfy your spouse's most pressing needs. Do this and you will resolve the conflict you are having.

As I write this, I can already hear the cries of frustration and disagreement. You may assume I am saying you should do whatever your spouse asks you to do regardless of your own needs and desires. But I did not say this, and I did not mean to imply it.

What I meant was that if you are in the middle of a conflict, stop and figure out what need your spouse is trying to get you to meet at the moment. Identify and satisfy this need and the conflict will be resolved.

Often, this doesn't mean sublimating your own needs and desires. But you may have to lay them aside temporarily so you can objectively determine your spouse's need. This is necessary, because as long as you are focused on your own needs you will not be able to respond effectively to your partner.

The most important key to resolving all marital conflict is to identify the needs of your partner and to clarify those needs to make sure you have them right. At least 60 percent of conflicts can be resolved by following these six conflict-resolution steps.

1. Consciously lay aside your own needs, desires, fears, and emotions.

THE KEY TO SOLVING ALL MARITAL CONFLICT   43

2. Stop doing what you are doing.
3. Look at your spouse.
4. Ask what your partner most needs at the moment.
5. Clarify that need.
6. Brainstorm and negotiate what needs to be done, if anything.

Follow this process and you will resolve the conflict. It's actually as easy as that—except for a couple of things that interfere.

Fear of not getting needs met is the major barrier to resolving conflict. There's a part of every person that screams out, "Hey, what about my needs?" This loud voice directs us away from our spouse's needs and on to getting our own needs met. What it takes to solve marital conflicts is for at least one person to quell this voice and focus on the needs of the other.

To quiet one's own voice isn't always easy. This is especially true if any of three conditions exist. The first is a pressing need a person feels for herself. The more urgently she feels her own need, the more difficult it is to lay it aside so she can listen to the needs of her spouse.

The second obstacle comes from negative feelings and/or moods. If a person is in a bad mood, stressed out, or intensely feeling something like anger, hurt, resentment, or jealousy, then listening to the needs of her spouse is very difficult.

The third obstacle also has to do with being stressed out or in a bad mood. These feelings tend to cause people to communicate their needs in ways that make their mates feel blamed, attacked, unappreciated, resentful, and angry.

As one of these conditions has a likelihood of existing at all times in any given marriage, it's necessary for at least one of the partners to consciously lay his or her own needs and feelings aside and to lead the other spouse through the six conflict-resolution steps. This is critical because as long as both people are communicating from their emotions, the conflict is likely to escalate.

When people are stuck in negative feelings, they are physiologically cut off from access to the logical part of their brains. They are likely to say all kinds of things that are hurtful and inflammatory. This being the case, someone has to take the lead to set aside emotions so she can lead the other back out of his emotions to deal logically with the situation at hand.

This process can take anywhere from one minute to several days. During that time, it's necessary for one person to have patience and to keep cool. It's very helpful if she can give her spouse as many messages as possible that he is capable, appreciated, respected, intelligent, sexy, and attractive. It's also helpful to give direct messages and to make requests like: "I love you and I care about you. I want to know what your needs are. Let's sit down and talk about them."

When her spouse does start to talk, it's likely that she will still have to consciously lay her feelings aside so she can listen. She needs to remember that when a person is responding emotionally, he is very likely to make statements that can cause her to feel blamed, hurt, and attacked. However, if she can stay detached and not get emotional, she will have a chance to listen to and clarify her mate's feelings and desires. Once this is done, there's a greater likelihood that both of them can calmly and rationally brainstorm and negotiate a solution to the conflict.

Love Potion

The next time you notice your spouse is upset, stop whatever you are doing and say, "Let's sit down and talk about whatever is on your mind." If you notice yourself starting to feel negative emotions during this process, in your own mind tell them loudly to "STOP AND WAIT!" Don't allow yourself the luxury of expressing your own feelings, desires, or needs until you have identified and clarified those of your spouse.

Each time you do this successfully you will be rewarded in several ways. The conflict will likely come to a resolution much more quickly and easily than if you focused on your own feelings, desires, and needs. A second reward will come from your mate's gratitude for responding to his or her needs in a loving way. The third reward will come from a rise in your self-esteem. Every time you consciously control your own emotions, your inner voice will praise you. This builds self-confidence.

Chapter 10

WHERE YOUR MARRIAGE FITS IN

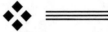

A ccording to a study of fifteen thousand couples done at the University of Minnesota, there are seven different kinds of marriages. Read the following marriage types out loud to your spouse. Discuss which category your marriage likely fits. Also talk about where you would like it to be.

1. *Devitalized:* These couples described themselves as very unhappy with all aspects of their relationships. This group has a high likelihood of divorce and comprises 40 percent of all marriages.

2. *Financially Focused:* In these marriages the couple's careers come before the relationship. Money, not love, is what holds the marriage together. This group accounts for 14 percent of all marriages.

3. *Conflicted:* These couples are dissatisfied with many, but not all, facets of their marriage. Conflicts are often left unresolved and pleasure is sought outside the relationship. This group also accounts for 14 percent of all marriages.

4. *Traditional:* These marriages are better off, with the couple reporting satisfaction in a number of areas. However, communication problems and sex-related difficulties are frequent complaints.

Ten percent of marriages fit into this category.

5. *Balanced:* These couples say they're moderately satisfied with their marriages. They tend to be strong in
problem-solving and communication, but money is
often a recurring problem. Eight percent of couples
belong to this category.

6. *Harmonious:* Highly satisfied couples make up this
category. They are happy with each other but often
complain about the children. If there are any problems or difficulties it's normally with the children.
This group accounts for 8 percent of marriages.

7. *Vitalized:* The couples in this category are very satisfied with their spouses and their marriages. In
addition, they have strong internal resources and are
good at resolving conflicts. Six percent of marriages
fall into this category.

Love Potion #6

Buy some massage lotion and some scented
candles. Give your spouse a surprise massage
tonight.

Chapter 11

GOOD MARRIAGES HAVE ONE CHEERLEADER, GREAT MARRIAGES HAVE TWO

Behind every successful man is a woman!" Like most clichés, this one has been around for so long because it's true.

In one of my books, *Smart Discipline for the Classroom*, I point out to teachers that success is dependent on encouragement, and that students cannot be successful in school unless they have someone to encourage them.

This also applies to marriages. In highly satisfying marriages, both partners encourage the other's hopes, dreams, and aspirations. And they do it on a daily basis. Encouragement becomes a habit.

Being your partner's greatest supporter is easy if you are still in the honeymoon phase of your marriage or if you agree wholeheartedly with your spouse's plans. The difficulty arises when you either don't agree with his or her aspirations or think your spouse is being anything from unrealistic to out-and-out stupid.

Naturally, when people share their plans with someone else, they often get caught up in their own excitement. At this time, they're very open and vulnerable. They're risking their inner-most dreams and ideas by sharing them with another person.

The other person, at this point, has several choices. One choice is to support and encourage, another is to listen and clarify, and another is to discourage. The first two choices strengthen relationships and the third destroys.

"Destroy" may seem a bit too strong, but it's a very real and major risk you take when you impede another's dreams. Even if you are right and the dream could never come true in a million years, the last thing you want to do to your spouse is point out why his idea won't work. In doing so, you will likely dissuade him from the dream—but at the same time you'll bruise your relationship badly. Do it enough times and you'll likely destroy it.

So what do you do when your spouse has a crazy idea and you are afraid she's about to "bet the farm" and lose it? The first thing to do is to listen and clarify. As enthusiastically as you can, ask all kinds of questions. Be interested and show that you understand how excited your partner is about her ideas. Say things like, "It sure seems like you are excited about this. Tell me more about it." And "Really? Tell me more. What would you do then?"

What we need most as human beings is to have someone listen to and understand us. When you give the gift of understanding and listening, you really don't have to fear what your mate will do with the idea at hand. Most likely, if it actually is a dumb idea, he'll realize this on his own within several days. Life has a way of throwing major hurdles up to dash crazy ideas before they get off the ground.

If this happens, and you've supported your spouse, she'll always remember and appreciate that support. If, on the other hand, your spouse does start to embark on an endeavor that you cannot support, you are in a much better position to say no if you've taken the time to fully understand the idea in the first place. Your spouse will appreciate you for listening and will now likely be open to listening to your thoughts on the subject.

But be careful with this. Encouragement or the lack thereof has a major bearing on the quality of a love relationship. For the most part, if you establish a habit of actively encouraging your spouse, you can look forward to a good deal of return encouragement. As well, you will likely have a spouse who'll achieve much greater things than he would have without your support.

Encouragement is an elixir of love. Give it in great measure and your love will grow accordingly. Withhold it and your love will diminish accordingly. It's truly your choice. Remember this, too: Whether you choose to encourage or discourage your spouse, he or she will always remember it!

Love Potion #7

Buy tickets to an event you know your spouse would enjoy. Tell your spouse you have the tickets but don't tell him or her what event they are for. Joke about the upcoming event but keep it a complete surprise. The anticipation should be as fun as the event itself!

Chapter 12

HOW TO ESTABLISH A POSITIVE VISION FOR YOUR MARRIAGE

In my work with people over the years, I've found one of the chief reasons people don't get what they want out of life is that they don't have a clear idea of what they want in the first place. This is just as true in marriages. If you don't have a crystal clear idea of what's important to you in your marriage, you will probably end up dissatisfied.

Knowing this, a couple seeking a long and happy marriage would be wise to take some time to establish a joint vision for their marriage. Here's how:

Step One: Set aside about an hour when you can spend some time uninterrupted. Turn off the television and agree to let the answering machine take messages. Fix yourself some snacks and put on some romantic music. Get out some paper and pencils.

Step Two: Separately, each of you should write positive statements about your marriage. Some examples are: "We are best friends"; "We are wonderfully affectionate"; "We like the same foods"; and "We have passionate sex."

Be sure to make each statement affirmative—instead of writing something like, "We don't put each other down," say, "We support and encourage each other."

Step Three: Add to your list positive statements you would like to be true about your marriage. State them in the same way you stated the ones you already feel are true. In other words, write them in the present tense, like: "We love to go dancing together." You can brainstorm the things you want on this list or choose from some of the following:

1. We are openly affectionate.
2. We are good at resolving conflicts.
3. We have positive attitudes.
4. We are both totally committed to making this marriage work.
5. We have strong communication skills.
6. We are very considerate of each other.
7. We are good at solving problems together.
8. We are creative.
9. We are financially organized and responsible.
10. We are flexible in our thinking.
11. We are best friends.
12. We are generous.
13. We love to give gifts to each other.
14. We are honest with each other.
15. We both do our fair share of household duties.
16. We are good at listening to each other.
17. We are great in the lovemaking department.
18. We are patient with each other.
19. We love to play together.
20. We are a romantic couple.
21. We have a high degree of awareness about our relationship.
22. We share laughter and delight on a daily basis.
23. We are sensitive to each other's needs.
24. We are spontaneous with each other.

Step Four: Share your list with your spouse. Put checks by the ones you have in common. Add statements from your spouse's list that you agree with but don't have on your list.

Step Five: Go back individually and put an "X" by the ones that are most important to you. Choose about seven items.

Step Six: Take a clean sheet of paper, and together with your spouse make one list. Be sure to include all seven items from each of your lists.

Step Seven: Put the list up somewhere you can't help but notice and read it on a daily basis.

One of the most powerful ways of getting what you want out of life is to define what you want and write it down. I don't know why this is, but there's almost something magical about writing down your goals. I can't recommend the completion of this exercise highly enough!

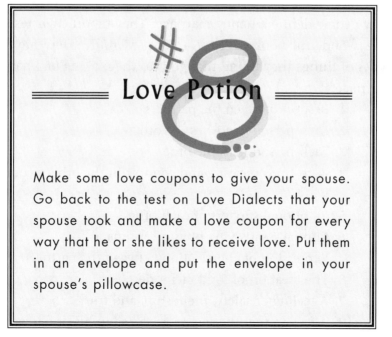

Love Potion #8

Make some love coupons to give your spouse. Go back to the test on Love Dialects that your spouse took and make a love coupon for every way that he or she likes to receive love. Put them in an envelope and put the envelope in your spouse's pillowcase.

Chapter 13

WHAT MAKES FOR A HAPPY MARRIAGE?

P eople have different ideas about what makes a happy marriage. But, for many, the question is one they have not asked themselves. Or at least if they have, they don't have a definitive answer in mind. So I think it's worthwhile to look at how other people define a happy marriage.

Judith Wallerstein and Sandra Blakeslee undertook the task of interviewing successful couples across America to find out how people define a happy marriage. They report their results in a wonderful book called *The Good Marriage*. Here are the types of things they found that go into the making of a happy marriage:

1. Respect between the partners
2. Each person cherishes the other
3. Each person likes the other
4. Each finds pleasure and comfort in the other's company
5. Emotional support of each other
6. Mutually satisfying physical intimacy
7. Expression of appreciation between the partners
8. The creation of fond memories
9. A feeling of safety, friendship, and trust
10. A feeling that the spouse is central to his or her world

11. An admiration of positive qualities such as honesty, generosity, decency, loyalty, and fairness
12. A strong sense of morality
13. The conviction that each person is worthy of being loved
14. A sense of reality, in that there are some problems but that they are surmountable
15. A view that each partner is special in some important regard
16. A sense that the marriage enhances each partner
17. The sense that there's a unique fit between each partner's needs and the spouse's willingness and ability to meet those needs
18. The sense that each partner is lucky to have the other
19. An equitable division of household tasks and child-rearing
20. A sense that the success of the marriage is attributable to both partners
21. An ability to express both positive and negative emotions
22. A shared view that the marriage takes constant attention and work

This is quite a list, isn't it? Surely any couple that has these things has a wonderful, blessed marriage!

However, it's important to note that such a marriage doesn't come about by accident. It takes years of dedicated work to bring this kind of relationship into existence. The good news is that it's certainly doable; in fact, millions of couples have just this kind of relationship. It does, though, take a major commitment on both parts to continually work on the marriage.

While I say that it takes a commitment from both people, please recognize that at any point in time the task of keeping the relationship together may fall more to one person than the other. At the time, it may seem unfair. But that's the way relationships are.

Sometimes one of the partners goes through a period of intense personal challenge, severely hampering his ability to contribute to the marriage. During these times, if the marriage is to survive, it's up to the other partner to keep the relationship together.

These are dangerous times in a relationship, dangerous in the sense that one person can come to feel so overburdened that she decides to end the relationship. Even the person facing personal challenges may decide he would be better off if the marriage ended. Some even come to believe the partner is the cause of the problems.

If marriages are to survive long enough to cultivate the wonderful characteristics listed earlier in this chapter, then both partners must agree to stick with the marriage until challenges can be met and overcome. Also in these times of great strife, the one factor that may save a marriage from dissolution is active participation in a faith community. Doing so cannot only provide avenues of encouragement for the couple to stay together but can provide the sustaining power of prayers from the faith community.

I think it prudent here to add a note of warning. In times of strife, couples often quit going to church, cut themselves off from their faith community, and cease all activities that are necessary to sustain their faith in God. Often this happens out of shame and sometimes out of depression. Whatever the reason for doing so, nothing could be worse. Having faith and a supporting faith community can make the difference between being able to keep a marriage together during times of trouble and ending up in divorce court. While it may take energy and courage that seemingly is unavailable in times where stress has used up all available resources, digging down deep to sustain your faith will, in the end, pay off hundredfold.

And the payoff comes in the long run, when surviving the rough times eventually strengthens the marriage and your faith. In a way, it's like a bone that breaks. When it heals, the fracture becomes the strongest part of the bone. So too, can a marriage survive difficult times. Once overcome, the problems may well become a source of strength to the marriage and to your faith.

In sum, your marriage can become one of great satisfaction and enduring love. But it will take lots of work and a commitment to staying in the marriage even through the rough times.

Love Potion

On a copy machine, make two copies of the list at the beginning of this chapter. Working separately, circle the items that you strongly feel already exist in your marriage. Put an "X" by the ones you feel need work. Discuss your results and brainstorm ways to work on the areas needing attention. Make a list of these things. Then pick three that each of you would be willing to do differently to improve your marriage. They can be different things and the selection should be totally up to each individual. As each of you put your chosen items into action, make sure to show your partner lots of appreciation. Express some appreciation right now.

Chapter 14

THE ESSENTIAL TASKS OF BUILDING A GOOD MARRIAGE

Drawing from the research of Dr. Judith Wallerstein in her book *The Good Marriage*, there are nine psychological tasks that couples must accomplish if they are to build a lasting and happy marriage. While these tasks aren't imposed by anyone else, they are necessary to the health of a marital relationship. Failure to undertake and complete these tasks successfully is to put the relationship on a course toward disaster.

The first task is for the partners to commit to each other—and at the same time detach themselves emotionally from their families of origin. In so doing they now must relate as a couple to their now extended families. In this manner, they begin to form their own unique family. During this time the partners help one another complete their transition into adulthood.

The second challenge or task is to build a sense of "us" through intimacy, while at the same time figuring out individual areas of autonomy. Building the relationship into a cohesive unit is the major challenge of this task, with both partners reaching agreement and feeling good about the new partnership. Yet, however tricky it may be, both people in the new union must also figure out for themselves how to maintain their individuality.

In the third task of marriage the couple faces bringing children into the family and the challenges of parenting. (This task, of course, won't apply to a couple who is unable to or chooses not to have children.) While having children is one of the most binding and satisfying tasks of the marriage, the real challenge comes in nurturing the relationship at the same time that you nurture the children.

Managing life's unpredictable adversities is the fourth task of marriage. Crisis- or stress-management is the name of the game. Life inevitably brings with it illnesses, job loss, relocations, natural disasters, and the deaths of family and friends. Despite the anguish these events can bring, the couple must learn how to get through them in a way that strengthens their love.

The fifth task is to figure out how to handle conflict, anger, and differences between the partners. The challenge is to confront these issues in such a way that each person still feels safe and cared for. For each to feel secure expressing anger and individual desires, both partners must reject all uses of physical and emotional abuse. Instead, functional ways of settling differences must be learned.

Establishing a mutually satisfying sex life is the sixth task of marriage. While this would seem the easiest of the tasks, it isn't. A sex life that meets the needs of both partners takes time, love, and sensitivity. This task is made more daunting by the influences of stress and hormonal changes at different times in the partners' lives. Because of these influences, much care must go into developing and maintaining a good sexual relationship.

Sharing laughter and delight is the seventh marriage task. Playfulness is essential for a vital marital relationship. Just as learning to handle the tough times is critical, it's just as important to have fun together. The ability to have fun together is what can keep the marriage alive and vibrant.

The eighth task is to learn how to encourage each other and provide the nurturing the other needs. Accomplishing this task strengthens the bond of love and is absolutely essential to a good marriage.

To accomplish the ninth task, couples must develop and recall a positive history of their togetherness. They must come to recall together the wonderful romantic and passionate times of their early relationship and use them to foster present-day romantic experiences. However, these recollections and desires to recreate emotions and experiences must be tempered with reality and the changes time has wrought.

Any couple able to meet these challenges and accomplish these tasks is sure to have a strong and vibrant marriage. In the following pages you will find information, suggestions, and exercises to help you accomplish these tasks so you can be happily married for a lifetime.

Love Potion #10

Either cook your spouse's favorite meal or take him or her out to eat at his or her favorite restaurant. Make it a surprise!

Chapter 15

PRAYER AND MARRIAGE

W hich do you think is a better way to predict the level of marital happiness—how often partners make love or how often they pray together? By the title of the chapter, I'm sure you know the answer. A Gallup poll confirms the answer is prayer.

Studies done on love and prayer reveal other interesting things. Partners who pray with their spouses: believe their spouses are more skilled lovers (62% vs. 49%); show more respect for each other (83% vs. 62%); agree on child-rearing issues (73% vs. 59%); and are more playful (56% vs. 45%). In addition, while individual prayer correlates with marital happiness, joint prayer correlates at a level twice as high. All these statistics are from the book *The 30 Secrets of Happily Married Couples* by Dr. Paul Coleman.

Coleman cites other interesting facts about prayer and marriage. Couples who have reconciled after one person wanted out of the marriage engage in joint prayer 85 percent of the time. In the study, other variables among recently reconciled couples were considered as well. These included frequency of sex, equality viewpoints, and conflict-resolution skills. While each of these had a bearing on successful reconciliation, none had the effect of joint prayer.

Another Gallup survey reveals marital stability and happiness are affected by the religious involvement of couples of all ages. According to research reported in the *Journal of Marriage and the Family,* the happiest marriages are the ones in which the couples are highly involved in observing their faith.

Just why partners who pray together stay happily married hasn't been established. However, research by priest and sociologist Andrew Greeley found there is a correlation between partners' passion for their faith and the passion they have for each other. In his research, he established that the more involved partners were in their spiritual life the more likely they were to report satisfying and intense sexual relationships.

Other research reported by Harold G. Koenig, MD (unfortunately, no relation to me) in his book, *The Healing Power of Prayer,* establishes a direct relationship between prayer and healing. What is interesting about his studies is that they scientifically verify a relationship between healing and prayer. As all love relationships need healing at one time or another, this is good to have verified.

The message of this chapter and of all these studies is that prayer and spiritual involvement enhance marital stability and happiness. Most couples, I would suspect, know this intuitively. But it's good to have it confirmed. And good to be reminded of it as well.

#11
Love Potion

Consider starting your day off together reading from a daily devotional book. You can find them at general and Christian bookstores. Starting your day together in prayer can help you be more cheerful, hopeful, energetic, decisive, reliable, tender, open, and loyal. Sounds like a good way to start your day, doesn't it?

Chapter 16

WRITE YOUR OWN TEN COMMANDMENTS OF MARRIAGE

I t's wise for couples to have rules and guidelines to go by. This is especially true if both people are aware of and committed to following the same set of rules.

To live without rules is to live in chaos. To live in chaos is to end up in divorce or loveless marriages. In enduring and happy marriages, there are always rules the couples have committed to follow. Many of these couples have never spoken of these rules, but know what they are.

Because rules are so vital to long-term happy marriages, I highly recommend that you identify, negotiate, write down, and commit to the rules you want to govern your marriage.

Having this set of rules helps marriages in several major ways. First, when temptations present themselves—as they always do—you will have a set of guidelines by which you can decide how to act. This is important, as temptations to have an affair often can be almost irresistible, especially when partners are feeling distant from their spouse. If you have a set of clear rules that you have solidly committed to, it's much easier to just say no.

Second, when partners take the time and effort to identify and commit to a set of rules to guide their marriage, it solidifies their relationship. Relationships benefit tremendously any time the partners take an action that expresses commitment for a life-time. Bolstering this commitment through rules provides partners with a great deal of security and helps love to endure and flourish.

Third, making written and spoken commitments to another person creates individual pride and strength. Again, this is important for meeting the challenges of temptation. Some temptations in life are so strong that they take a lot of willpower to overcome. Commitment to a clearly defined set of guidelines can give couples the boost of willpower to meet such challenges. As human beings, once we make commitments, we are very reluctant to break them. This is especially so if they are commitments of our own making.

Fourth, commitment to a set of personal marital command-ments will help you treat your spouse in loving ways even when you are tired, stressed out, irritable, depressed, angry, cranky, or feeling unloved. It's much easier to be a loving spouse when you are feeling great and all is well than to act in loving ways when you are down. It's during the bad times that having a set of guidelines for acting appropriately can really help. They can make the difference between asking for a hug or some "alone time" and screaming and assigning blame.

Fifth (and last), having a strong set of identifiable guidelines will make your marriage a great model for your children. Having and following your set of marital commandments will clearly show your children that both of you are totally committed to making each other feel capable, appreciated, respected, intelli-gent, sexy, and attractive. You can be assured that your children will go out into the world looking to establish a similar relation-ship, one in which they can also become happily married for a lifetime.

#12
Love Potion

Plan a weekend getaway to one of your favorite spots. Take a notebook with you. During the weekend, brainstorm guidelines that each of you might like to see incorporated into your personal Ten Commandments of Marriage. Feel free to flip through this book to give you some ideas. Before the weekend is out, identify, negotiate, and write out your set of marital commandments. When you get home, use your creativity to display them for all to see. (Hint: We human beings are better able to stick to our commitments if everyone around us knows what we have committed to.)

Chapter 17

KISS AND TELL: PART 1

How well do you really know your spouse?

Most married people answer this question with something like, "Very well. In fact, I know my spouse better than she knows herself."

No matter how well you know your spouse, there's a lot more to know. The good thing is that happily married partners say they never tire of getting to know their spouses better.

The chapters titled "Kiss and Tell" will be devoted to helping you discover more about your spouse. You can expect this process of discovery to be an extraordinarily powerful one. Not only will you be pleased to uncover a number of exciting things about your spouse, but you will also, in the process of asking and listening, bolster and cement the bond of love between you.

In several places in this book I say that for love to flourish, each person must feel capable, appreciated, respected, intelligent, sexy, and attractive. One of the most powerful ways I know for couples to communicate these things to each other is by asking important questions and attentively listening to the answers.

So, in the "Kiss and Tell" chapters, I've included questions for you to ask your spouse. The more you ask, the better you will come to know your partner and the better he or she will feel about himself or herself. Both of you will benefit by increased feelings of love and compassion.

KISS AND TELL INSTRUCTIONS

1. Flip a coin to see who goes first. The winner decides whether to Kiss or Tell first.
2. The Kisser gives the Teller a kiss (preferably passionate) and picks a question to ask.
3. The Kisser follows the Rules of Listening (see chapter 20, "The Rules of Listening").
4. The Teller answers the questions to the best of his or her ability.
5. Switch roles. The new Kisser can choose to ask the same question or a different one.
6. Use your sense of humor. Laughter and all forms of encouragement are strongly suggested.

KISS AND TELL QUESTIONS

1. What attracted you to me the first time we met?
2. What is a favorite tradition of yours from your childhood?
3. Do you ever have crazy thoughts? If so, what do you do about them?
4. What do you fear most?
5. Have you ever been able to overcome a fear? If so, how did you do it?
6. What do you think are your best features? Your worst?

7. If you could have one super power, what would you choose and why?

8. What is the smartest thing you have ever done outside of marrying me?

9. What was your most embarrassing moment in childhood? How did it affect your life?

10. Would you rather continue doing what you are doing with most of your time, or would you rather do something else? Why or what?

11. Which feelings are easy for you to express and which are hard? Why?

12. What thoughts does the statement "It's more important to understand than to be understood" bring to your mind? How do you think it applies to marriage?

#13
Love Potion

Make love in every room of your house. Don't forget your closets, laundry room, and staircases. Be creative. Take your time. Make each time and place an unforgettable experience. Take turns creating the experience for different rooms. Name the room and time and set a date to meet there.

Chapter 18

THE SEVEN STAGES OF MARRIAGE

It's important to know that there are stages in marriage. Knowing this allows us to realize that we aren't alone in the challenges we are facing, and that each phase will indeed pass if we have the patience to persevere.

Following is a description of seven stages identified by Maxine Rock in her book *The Marriage Map*. Much of what we're trying to do here is discover how to meet the challenges of these stages.

Stage one is the *honeymoon* period. During this phase, the couple derives intense satisfaction from the relationship. Each partner is blind to the other's faults, or either minimizes or dismisses them as trivial. Emotionally and sexually the couple is on a natural high. The average length of this period of marriage is two years. Some report their honeymoon ended before they got home from the trip; others say their honeymoon lasted several years.

Stage two is the *compromise* period. The blinders come off, and each partner becomes acutely aware of the other's faults. What a disappointment it can be to learn your partner is far from the perfect person you thought you married. Some of the faults annoy, others seem hurtful. The couple, during this stage, starts to negotiate change. Couples that successfully make it through the compromise stage ask for change and agree to do some changing themselves. Others, faced with all their partner's faults as well as their own, decide to flee the marriage. This stage normally lasts between two and seven years.

Stage three is the period of *reality struggles*. Reality sets in during this stage of marriage. While the couple has negotiated for and gotten some change, each partner realizes that the other is unlikely to change significantly. This is also the time when more bonding takes place, as the partners come to accept each other, blemishes and all. Children and financial dependence also serve to strengthen the marital bonds during this stage. This normally represents the fifth to the tenth years of marriage.

Stage four is called the *time of decisions*. Having come to face that each marriage partner has faults, each must decide whether to continue in the marriage. At this point, they start to weigh each other's good points against their flaws and whether the good makes it worth putting up with the bad. This stage usually occupies the tenth to the fifteenth years of marriage.

Stage five is called *separation*. This is a time when partners push away from each other. Some divorce, some separate, and others distance themselves emotionally. This stage is extremely painful. It ends when and if the couples enter into discussions on what changes each wants and is willing to make in order to make the marriage work. Given the willingness to engage in this process, the love grows and strengthens.

Those that last through the first five stages of marriage enter into the sixth stage, which is called *together again*. In this stage the couple comes to final terms with their differences and decides to live with them no matter what. Talk of divorce or separation is set aside in favor of realization that this union is for life. Chances for love and growth in the marriage are greatly enhanced when this decision is reached. Attention now turns to enhancing the marriage and committing to the long term. This stage usually occupies the seventeenth to the twentieth years of marriage.

Stage seven is called *new freedom*. Couples in this stage breathe a sigh of relief. They no longer have to pour so much energy into changing or making the marriage work. They enter into a natural flow of being together. Neither worries much any more about what the other is thinking or doing. Trust, compassion, communication, and support flow freely between the partners. This is also a time when the spouses, secure in their marriage, explore new ways of fulfilling themselves. This stage, which normally occupies the twentieth to twenty-fifth years, is considered by many as the beginning of the best years of marriage.

Last comes what is called *ongoing growth*. This isn't a stage, as it has no end. Rather, it's a time in the marriage when the couple has successfully completed the stages and now is free to expand both their love and personal horizons. It's the time when both can relax and enjoy each other and their lives. This is the rich reward for sticking out the tough times and keeping the marriage together.

According to Rock, every marriage goes through these stages—no exceptions. However, if it's a remarriage, couples quickly go through the initial stages and catch up to where they left off in previous marriages. The stages then progress at a normal rate. If you get married when you are older, you quickly catch up to your peers' relationships and then progress at a normal rate.

#14
Love Potion

Read the stages out loud to your partner when you are driving somewhere. Discuss which stages you have gone through and what stage you think your marriage is in now. Discuss why you think it's helpful to know about the stages of marriage. When you stop the car make out with your spouse for at least two minutes.

Chapter 19

THE ART OF SETTLING ARGUMENTS: PART 1

C onflicts come up in all marriages. They simply cannot be avoided. Even before getting married, couples have spats over jealousy and in-law issues. After they get married they move on to arguments that arise over sex and communication. Then come arguments over the handling of household tasks and children.

At every turn in the first twenty years of marriage, all types of arguments crop up. The subjects change, but the need to deal with conflicts in ways that both resolve the problem and preserve the marriage remains constant.

Most couples come to a conflict-resolution style through trial and error. This isn't so much by choice or design but rather because they aren't presented with any resources on problem-solving. If they were, I suppose many would opt to learn the art of settling arguments peacefully. Wouldn't you?

The first skill is both the easiest and the most difficult. This is the art of listening. On the one hand, listening is easy. All it takes is for one person to be quiet, be attentive, look at the person who is talking, ask pertinent questions, and clarify what the other person is saying. This is an easy process that takes little training to learn.

Listening is made difficult by the emotions we feel. Often in marital communication, one person will talk and the listener will become highly defensive and angry over what is said. This is a major problem, because there must be a discussion of the issues for any argument to be resolved successfully. Both parties must be able to clearly state their position and feel that the other person has listened and understood.

If both partners can state their positions and feel heard and understood, resolving the problem will likely be much easier. In fact, between 70 and 80 percent of all arguments can be resolved without any action having to be taken if this process is success-fully completed. This is because one of the primary human needs each person has is to be listened to and understood.

So large is this need that in the United States we spend bil-lions of dollars annually to hire people to listen to us. We call them psychologists, social workers, counselors, ministers, and therapists. Why do we pay them so much? Well, it's because we deeply need to be listened to and understood; yet, we don't have people in our family willing or able to do so.

When it comes down to it, if you can learn how to listen to each other, you probably can and will have a very happy, stable marriage. So powerful is the gift of listening that it can help you build and maintain one of the most satisfying marriages imagi-nable. Couples that don't learn this skill will have a very tough time of it, and their satisfaction in the marriage will diminish markedly over time.

Enough said about how important listening is. Let's move on to how to develop the art of listening in a marriage.

Chapter 20

THE RULES OF LISTENING

To develop the art of listening, you must practice and follow a few rules. The rules are simple, but you must adhere to them for successful and satisfying communication to take place.

If you are the person listening, you must:

1. Agree to a time to stop what you are doing and listen.
2. Maintain eye contact with your spouse.
3. Ask nonjudgmental questions.
4. Clarify what is being said and ask if it's accurate.
5. Re-clarify if necessary.
6. Refrain from expressing your own thoughts and feelings.
7. Refrain from offering solutions.
8. Refrain from blaming.
9. Refrain from offering advice.
10. Refrain from getting defensive.

If you are the person talking, you must:

1. Request that your spouse take time to listen to you.
2. State your views as completely as possible.
3. State your feelings.

4. Refrain from blaming.
5. Refrain from criticism, sarcasm, and put-downs.

The listener has the lion's share of the responsibility. However, in order for the discussion to come off successfully, both parties must adhere to their set of rules. Once the talker agrees that she has been fully understood, the listener can request that his views be heard. In this case, partners switch roles and the process begins again.

While much training can be done on the particulars of listening, such as how to clarify and how to ask nonjudgmental questions, I don't think most people need it. Knowing how to clarify and ask questions isn't the problem. The problem lies in keeping emotions in check and refraining from breaking rules six through ten. This takes practice and self-control. To become good at it takes years, and both parties need to exercise patience.

It should be pointed out, too, that the person talking also must practice how he shares his emotions. While it's okay to express how you feel, you must learn to stop short of blaming your spouse for your feelings.

One way of doing this is by using ABC statements. In ABC statements you use this format: "When you do A in situation B, I feel C."

In reality it might go something like, "When you sit and watch television while I am cleaning house, I feel angry." Or, "When you give me the silent treatment because I don't agree with you about something, I get angry and frustrated."

By using such a format, you avoid blame, criticism, sarcasm, and put-downs. You also gain a means for making your message clear.

It's still possible for the listener to feel blame despite the ABC format, even when there's no intention of assigning blame. This is where self-control comes in. Even if you're feeling you're being blamed, you need to refrain from expressing it. Rather, you must stick to the role of listener and clarify what is being said and felt.

The best way of doing this is to simply "mirror" back what your spouse has said. For example, "What I hear you saying is that when I sit and watch television while you clean the house, you get angry. Is that right?" Or, "What I hear you saying is that when I give you the silent treatment when you disagree with me, you get angry and frustrated. Is that right?" If it isn't quite right, then your spouse should rephrase his or her thoughts and feelings and you should clarify them once again.

All of this takes patience and practice. But, wow, is it worth it! If you can master the art of listening, your chance for a satisfying marriage dramatically increases. Remember, though, there probably still will be times when emotions override your spouse's ability to practice the Rules of Listening.

#15

Love Potion

Pick out something you would like to discuss. Choose something that isn't too emotionally charged. You may even want something that has no emotional charge to it whatsoever, such as something happening in the news. Take turns being the listener and the talker. First, practice following the Rules of Listening as stated in this chapter. Then discuss the rules you could have broken and how this would have affected the conversation. Take a break and have a wrestling match. Tickling is encouraged!

Chapter 21

THE ART OF SETTLING ARGUMENTS: PART 2

A s I pointed out in chapter 16, arguments often dissipate without anyone having to do anything other than listen to and understand the other's point of view. The process can seem magical. Each and every time it's successfully completed, the love bond between partners is strengthened.

However, there are other times when just listening and understanding aren't enough. Decisions must be made and actions carried out. How to do this in a way that preserves and strengthens your marriage is the subject of this chapter.

Some people fear that by bringing up areas of conflict they are putting their marriage at risk. This isn't the case. Couples that learn to deal with discord successfully are the ones likely to stay happily married. Avoiding conflict leads to problems. The longer negative feelings and thoughts are repressed, the stronger they become. Then they are likely to come out with such emotion that it's difficult for either person to deal with them rationally. It's far better to deal with differences as they come up than to allow them to fester.

So let me suggest a problem-solving formula. If you follow it, you will be able to solve virtually any problem that comes your way as a couple. However, it is absolutely essential to preface this process with both of you expressing your views and feelings until both believe the other understands to the best degree possible.

Keep in mind that I am not saying you must agree; rather, you should understand each other's thoughts and feelings. Once mutual understanding has been reached, employing the problem-solving strategy will be easy for you—and highly effective.

THE PROBLEM-SOLVING STRATEGY

The first step is to agree to what the problem is. To do this, it's necessary first to lay aside any feelings of blame. This should be fairly easy to do if you have made the effort to listen to and understand each other's point of view.

Some problems are small and easy to identify. Others are more complex and have many elements to them. For example, deciding where to go out to eat is one thing, solving child-rearing problems another. (However, for some couples, agreeing on a place to eat can be a major problem.) If the problem is a more complex one, break it down into smaller parts you can deal with one at a time. By breaking problems down, couples can avoid becoming overwhelmed.

One example of this might be dealing with financial problems, which have many facets to them and are also highly emotionally charged. After discussing the problem using the Rules of Listening, you would break it down into smaller parts, something like credit-card management, ways to spend less, ways to bring in more money, bill-paying, and checkbook-management. Then tackle the smaller, easier issues first; once those are solved, work on the more difficult ones.

Once you have agreed what the problem is, you are ready to go on to the second step—brainstorming solutions. While the process is a fairly simple one, NASA developed some guidelines that work well and are used in businesses from Microsoft to Disney. Couples can put them to use just as effectively.

The Rules of Brainstorming

1. Ideas should be written down.
2. Any idea can be suggested.
3. No idea should be evaluated during the process, verbally or nonverbally (in other words, no making faces!).
4. Be creative (silly ideas can have wonderful potential for opening the door to great solutions).
5. Stick with it when you get stuck. Use humor to get going again.

This process should be a fun one, and it has the potential to provide solutions you may have otherwise missed. It can also relieve tension and give you a sense of hope and teamwork.

Step three in the problem-solving strategy is to agree on a specific solution you both would be willing to try. This may take some compromise. It may also take combining two or three ideas from your brainstorming session. To ease the process of deciding, go back over the ideas from the brainstorming session and mark all that appeal to either of you. Then identify any ideas both of you like and can agree upon.

If there's no obvious agreement between the two of you, pick an idea you would both be willing to try for a set period of time, after which you will come back and assess the results. The key to this step is agreeing on a specific solution, with specific actions clearly assigned and agreed upon. And these agreements must take into account both people's needs rather than just one person's (please see chapter 1 on principles of harmony).

Step four is to follow up on solutions that will be enacted over time. Some problems are short in duration, and once a solution is agreed upon and put into place there's no need for further discussion; an example of this might be deciding where to go on vacation. Other problems, such as financial problems, need long-term solutions.

If the problem you are solving is long-term in nature, decide when you will come back to assess it. When you do return to the discussion, talk about whether the idea is working. If it is, discuss whether there are any ways to improve on it. If the solution isn't working, go back to the third step and pick another solution you are both willing to try. If you can't find one, hold another brainstorming session.

At every step in this process it's critical to respect each other's ideas and feelings. Blame and anger must be avoided if the problem-solving strategy is to produce results.

Every bit of time and effort a couple puts into learning and employing the problem-solving process is worthwhile. Each time it's successfully completed, your love will grow and your marriage will strengthen.

Please note: Some marriage problems are unsolvable. The best you can hope for is to find ways to cope with them and accept their presence.

#16

Love Potion

Set aside time to practice the problem-solving strategy. Pick a problem you would like to solve, but start out with something that isn't highly emotionally charged. In other words, in the beginning stay away from issues that lead to angry or hurt feelings. Have some fun with the strategy. Get out some snacks and put on your favorite music. Plan to make love when you get done.

THE ART OF SETTLING ARGUMENTS: PART 3

According to the Ohio State University Medical Center, negative behaviors during marital fights affect the immune system. These negative behaviors not only adversely affect health—they affect the relationship as well. The behaviors identified in the study included put-downs, sarcasm, interruptions, excuses, and the denial of responsibility.

This isn't to say that fighting is bad. Quite the contrary. Couples who learn to confront and resolve their differences have much happier marriages than couples who avoid arguing.

If you are like most couples, you likely have the same arguments over and over. And if you are like most couples, your arguments most often fall into five different categories: fairness, children, commitment, money, and sex.

The way couples argue is critically important to the marriage. Some have fights that lead to solutions and intimacy. Others have arguments that lead to further harshness and division.

Couples who stay happily married learn to follow these rules:

- Bring up the problem as soon as possible, before it becomes enormous.
- Talk only about the issue at hand. No "throwing in the kitchen sink."

- Stick to the present. No dredging up the past.
- The use of definitives isn't allowed (e.g., "never" and "always").
- Verbal and physical threats aren't allowed.
- Hitting, slapping, and any displays of violence are strictly forbidden.
- State needs and wants as specific requests for different behaviors.
- If the fight escalates, take at least thirty minutes alone to cool off. If one of you is really "stuck" in negative feelings, a cooling-off period of several days may be needed. If tempers still flare, outside help should be sought before broaching the issue again.

Couples that follow these rules have a much better chance of staying happily married than couples that consistently break them. But it isn't easy to follow them, and there's a very good reason why.

When you feel extreme emotions such as anger, hurt, and fear, your brain starts to shut down communication between the logical brain and the "old brain" that's directed by emotions. The old brain is the one that causes us to run like heck if a car is coming at us. For the sake of preservation, it doesn't want you to think about running; it just wants you to run!

This old brain also kicks into action when we argue. As we feel anger, hurt, and fear, it overrides the logical brain and tells us to either fight or flee. So, we do what it tells us. This is why it's so critical that the first rule of fighting be followed. If we can resolve issues early on before they get out of hand, then our feelings will not be strong enough to stir our old brain into action.

The rules of fighting require practice and patience. Arguing in such a way that you achieve both intimacy and resolution is far more of an art than a science. As such, it takes years to perfect. Along the way you will experience both success and disappointments, but it will be worth the effort.

#17

Love Potion

The next time your spouse unknowingly offends you in some minor way, let go of it. Don't even mention it. Just give him or her a break. Pat yourself on the back for being a kind-hearted person and do something extra nice for him or her that day.

Chapter 23

EVERY MARRIAGE NEEDS A HENRY KISSINGER

All couples have problems. While some have more than others, conflicts are present throughout all marriages. The couples who go on to be happily married for a lifetime find ways to address and resolve conflicts before they get out of hand.

Every marital conflict has development stages. First, someone says or does something that the other person doesn't like. Either it hurts the other person's feelings or it's objectionable for some reason. Second, the offended person decides whether or not to communicate his discontent. Some problems are resolved at this stage simply by the person dropping the problem. However, even when a person decides not to mention his discontent, it may fester and come out indirectly.

If the problem gets communicated, the third stage begins. This is the initial response stage. If the problem is clearly stated, the response time will likely be short. The less clearly it is communicated the longer the response will take. Regardless of the response time, the marriage partner makes a decision as to how he will respond. This choice is greatly affected by the way the problem was communicated. If it was expressed in a positive way, then he will have a positive response. The opposite will usually occur if the problem was communicated negatively.

Once the problem has been stated and an initial response made, the conflict enters into a negotiation phase. Here couples identify the way they would like to resolve the conflict. Each person clarifies how he views the problem, what should be done about it, and by whom. Eventually, partners will either come to some sort of resolution or lay the problem aside without resolving it. If the latter happens, the problem will likely arise again and again until it's finally resolved or the couple gets a divorce.

In happy marriages, of course, the problems are resolved so both partners' needs are satisfied. Neither partner is willing to resolve conflicts in ways that only satisfy the needs of one person. Rather, solutions are found and agreed upon that both not only can live with, but feel good about.

The negotiation phase requires that one person in the marriage act the part of Henry Kissinger. That is, someone needs to initiate the negotiation process and to move it along to a successful conclusion. Certainly both partners have to participate in the process, but one will have to initiate and facilitate the negotiation. This takes one person laying aside her own feelings and needs for the moment. Until this happens, both people are likely to stay "in their feelings," and chances for resolution will be minimal.

To play the impartial role of Henry Kissinger, she can say, "Why don't we talk about this. Tell me how you are feeling. Tell me what you think should be done." Doing this greatly enhances the chances that her spouse will be willing to enter into the negotiation phase. If "Kissinger" can first listen to and clarify feelings and the desired solutions of her spouse before proffering any of her own, the couple will be well on the way to successful conflict resolution.

This isn't easy to do because of fear that one of the partner's feelings, needs, and desires will be trod upon. But, in happy marriages, at least one person makes the effort to control her fears and lay them aside. This sends her spouse an underlying message that, "I care about you enough to lay aside my own feelings and desires so I can listen to yours; you are so important to me that I want to make sure your needs are being met."

Doing this for your partner is a great gift to both of you. Each time you do it, you prevent blow-ups and you increase the chances of an outcome that fills your needs as well.

In real life, one person in a relationship takes on the Kissinger role most often. It's like sex. In every relationship, one person most often initiates it. This isn't always desirable. As in sex, it's better for the relationship if both people share the roles. However, realistically speaking, one person will always be the chief initiator. So, if you are the one who most often is willing to take on the role of being Henry Kissinger, be pleased and pat yourself on the back. It's a great role to have in a marriage. It will contribute to the peace, harmony, and longevity of the marriage.

Love Potion

Establish a nonverbal sign with your spouse that says, "Let's talk. I'm willing to listen to you. Tell me what your feelings and desires are." Try this sign out the next time your spouse is upset about something.

Also, go shopping for a mask of Henry Kissinger. Hide it and wear it the next time your spouse is upset. A little humor can go a long way in settling disputes. Come to think of it, a Nixon mask might work just as well.

Chapter 24

How to Get Your Point Across Without Using Criticism

The most corrosive thing you can do in a love relationship is to criticize your spouse frequently. Infrequent criticism probably won't sink a relationship. A steady diet of it, though, will damage a love relationship beyond repair.

When I talk about this in my seminars, people want to know how they're supposed to let someone know they're displeased without coming across as being critical. This is a good question, because for a happy marriage to exist the partners must be able to negotiate change. If this possibility doesn't exist, the marriage will end—either emotionally or in divorce court.

A couple of ways of resolving conflict and negotiating change have already been suggested in other chapters. In this chapter we will deal with a slightly different strategy for negotiating change. I call it "Constructive Complaining."

There are three guidelines for making a complaint constructive. The first is to make the complaint specific. It can't be global in nature. For example, it's okay to say, "I dislike it when you come home late without calling me." It isn't okay to say, "You are always late and you never call me."

Second, in a constructive complaint you tell your spouse how you feel. Most often you can distill your feelings down into one or two words. Something like the following will work:

"When you stay on the Internet all night, I feel lonely and unappreciated."

Third, constructive complaints are short. No more than a sentence or two is allowed. Following this guideline will help you keep from blaming, which has no place in a constructive complaint.

In a constructive complaint you can also follow the ABC format I described in chapter 21, "The Art of Settling Arguments: Part 2." To recap this format, you plug your feelings and thoughts into the following formula: "When you do A in situation B, I feel C." It would come out something like this: "When you don't get the things at the grocery store that I put on the list, I feel angry."

A constructive complaint is very different from a criticism. Criticism usually assigns blame and is less than specific. When people use criticism they also tend to go on and on. Criticism is emotionally charged and often leads to a fight. Rarely does it lead to a successful resolution; rather, it often leads to hurt feelings and thoughts of revenge.

Worse than criticism is criticism capped with contempt. Contempt is found in statements that add insult to the criticism, such as, "Look at our house. You are such a slob." Or, statements like, "You'd spend half the weekend in bed if I let you. I've never met someone as lazy as you. No wonder we have financial problems."

Marital-communication research has established that couples who criticize or express contempt will likely divorce within three years. This should alarm you if criticism is part of the way you communicate with your spouse. The good news is that it's possible to jettison the criticism in favor of constructive complaints. To do so takes a commitment, some self-control, and lots of practice.

Let me end the subject of criticism with this analogy. When I went to the dentist to have my semi-annual cleaning, the hygienist asked me the question every dental hygienist asks when she gets done cleaning your teeth—"Do you floss?"—to which I answered sheepishly, "Well, most of the time, but perhaps not as much as I should." She replied, "Well, you only need to floss if you want to keep your teeth." The same applies here—you only need to get rid of criticism if you want to keep your marriage together!

Love Potion

The next time you want to complain about something, stop yourself. Instead, write out your complaint. Follow the guidelines for making a complaint constructive. Tell your spouse that you have a constructive complaint and ask him or her to listen to it and "mirror" it back to you before he or she responds to it. In other words, your spouse is to say something like, "What I hear you saying is that when I leave my clothes on the floor you get angry. Is that right?"

Once he or she "mirrors" the complaint back, express your appreciation for hearing you correctly. Then ask if it would be okay to schedule a brainstorming session to help resolve the problem (see chapter 21). Reward yourself for doing a good job by going out for ice cream or gourmet coffee.

Chapter 25

NINE WAYS SUCCESSFUL COUPLES EXPRESS THEIR LOVE DAILY

D r. John Gottman, University of Washington psychology professor, studied more than two thousand couples and reported the results in his book *Why Marriages Succeed or Fail.*

One thing he found was that stable couples had at least five times more positive interactions than negative ones—a 5-to-1 ratio. I think it's safe to assume that the greater this ratio was, the better the marriage.

He also found that couples used a variety of ways to interact positively. Here are the nine categories of positive interaction Dr. Gottman reported.

SHOW INTEREST

One way you can show love is by showing an active interest in your partner's activities. This is done chiefly by taking the time to ask questions about his or her day. It's also important to stop doing whatever you are doing while you ask the questions and focus on your mate, and to ask appropriate follow-up questions like, "And then what happened?" A positive attitude that reflects a sincere interest is essential.

EXPRESS AFFECTION

Obvious expressions of love (in ample quantities) such as sexual intercourse, hugs, kisses, and endearments are necessary in marriage. Smaller expressions of affection are also meaningful in a good love relationship. These can include holding hands, curling up on the couch together, spooning, and playing "footsie." These and other little ways of expressing your affection can add up to a satisfying relationship.

EXPRESS CONSIDERATION

During major holidays, couples are normally fairly good at showing they care. Happily married couples are good also at expressing how much they care on a daily basis. They do so through small, considerate actions, such as calling to say hi when they know their spouse has a tough day ahead, doing one of the household chores that she normally does, stopping to buy their spouse's favorite treat, or doing something the spouse loves to do even though they'd rather be doing something else. Rarely do partners in happy, longstanding marriages point to the big things their spouses did for them over the years. Rather, they have loving recollections of the pattern of small acts of love.

SHOW APPRECIATION

People choose their mate in large part because of the way they feel when they're with that person. And one of the ways they feel when they're feeling loved is appreciated. Appreciation not only makes a person feel loved, but it also increases the likelihood of encouraging and expanding the very quality being appreciated. The more you appreciate your mate for doing something, the more he or she will want to continue doing it. The next chapter addresses appreciation in more detail.

SAY YOU ARE SORRY

Loving people often know when they've said or done something to hurt their mate. Sometimes they know it a fraction of a second after they've made an insensitive remark. Once said, it's too late to take it back—but not too late to apologize.

Saying you are sorry is tough for a lot of people. Why this is, I'm not sure. If it's easy for you, then you probably do so whenever needed. If it's hard for you, then you'll have to find the courage. The good thing is that when you do apologize, most spouses are extremely appreciative. Saying you are sorry for something may be just the start of making amends, but it's a good start.

EXPRESS EMPATHY

One form of empathy is listening to your partner's trials and tribulations and expressing your understanding and concern. This is good to do on a regular basis.

Another kind of empathy puts yourself in your spouse's shoes. To do this, you must, of course, be sincere in your desire to express compassion. Show that you truly want to know what it's like to be in your spouse's place at the moment. Ask as many questions as possible—if your spouse is ready to talk—to get a complete picture of what is being experienced and the resulting feelings. When you think you have enough information, express to your spouse the empathy you have for his or her struggles. Clarify how you think it must feel to go through what your spouse is going through.

This is a wonderful gift to give someone you love. Not everyone can do it, but it's well worth the effort if you can.

SHOW ACCEPTANCE AND UNDERSTANDING

It's a great relief to have someone who accepts you the way you are. Especially if this person can take what you say and do without criticizing or badgering you about it. This is a form of unconditional love.

I don't think it's possible for couples to show unconditional love for each other all of the time—or even most of the time. But it's wonderful to have it even for short periods of time. Sometime, when you know your spouse really needs it or when nothing particular is going on, tell your spouse how much you love him/her, that he/she doesn't need to change a thing for you to love them and that you foresee your love lasting through all eternity. Do this over a romantic dinner or even when you are eating breakfast one morning.

BE PLAYFUL

Couples sometimes wonder if their teasing and silliness is normal or if one day they need to grow up. The truth is that we all have an inner child that wants to come out and play. For most people, the only safe place to play is with their spouse. Teasing, sharing personal jokes, and having an uproarious time together isn't only okay but it will strengthen your love bond. The only caution is that the fun you are expressing must be fun to both partners. If not, then that particular expression of playfulness should be avoided.

SHARE LAUGHTER AND DELIGHT

There are many things to both laugh about and be delighted with in a day's time. Loving couples look for and share these things with each other. The more you use your sense of humor and share your joy with your spouse the easier life and love will come.

#20 Love Potion

In other chapters, I talk about ways to resolve conflicts successfully. Yet, the very best way to resolve conflict is to not have it in the first place. And the best way I know to reduce the number of conflicts you and your spouse have is for each of you to feel full of love. When a person feels filled with love, potential conflicts seem to melt away. So, express your love to your mate at least five times a day. Use as many of the different kinds of love expressions as possible. Here's my guarantee: Expressing your love five times a day will keep the divorce lawyers away!

WHAT EVERY PERSON NEEDS FOR LOVE TO FLOURISH

L ove is a fascinating subject. To one degree or another, it interests almost everyone. It isn't surprising, then, that scientists and researchers have put a lot of effort into studying it.

One of the things researchers have clearly established about love relationships is that there's a direct correlation between the love a person feels for someone and how important and worthwhile he feels in the eyes of the loved one. Put another way, the more appreciation you show your spouse, the more he or she will reciprocate.

This makes a lot of sense. It's a great human need to feel valuable, needed, and appreciated. This is evident at work. When employees are asked what their employer can do to improve the workplace, one of the most common answers is they can show more appreciation.

Appreciation is important because our sense of self-worth is very much tied to the feedback we get from other people. Books on self-esteem state that we shouldn't rely on other people for our self-worth. But the fact is we do. Don't you have a need to feel important to those around you? How do you know whether the people around you value you? One of the ways has to be through their expressions of appreciation.

People need to be recognized and appreciated for their positive qualities and contributions. If in a love relationship, they will reciprocate by expressing love back. This process makes appreciation a true elixir of love.

You probably already know this, yet I think we all need to be reminded over and over again. Everyday life can take its toll; we get so busy that we don't get around to showing appreciation to those we love.

Not expressing appreciation to your mate can be deadly to your relationship. It's like neglecting to water and fertilize your plants. If you don't do it, they will wither and die. So will love. Just like plants, love needs to be nourished on a regular basis (daily is best).

Unfortunately, the chief complaint in many marriages is that individuals feel unappreciated and taken for granted. But in happy marriages, both partners act daily to make sure this doesn't happen. Rather, they go out of their way to show appreciation.

So, what are the best ways to let your loved one know he or she is important to you and appreciated by you? There are two. One is to simply say "thank you." I don't think you can say thank you enough in a marriage. Never have I had someone in my office complain that her spouse says thank you too often. And it's important to say thank you for the small things, the mundane tasks that are done on a daily basis. The more you do it, the more you strengthen the love bond. Keep in mind, too, that expressing appreciation for small things may count more than the expected appreciation for the larger things.

Another is to compliment. Expressing your admiration for a person's personal qualities goes a long way toward making someone feel loved. Complimenting how well someone does a particular thing is also valuable in building and maintaining a relationship.

Three things will happen when you take the time and effort to express appreciation to the person you love. First, that person's love for you will grow. Second, your love for that person will grow. Third, the behaviors and qualities you focus on will increase. These should provide you with ample motivation to make sure you express appreciation on a daily basis.

#21

Love Potion

The following are the top twenty-five behaviors married couples engage in together. Each can be both appreciated and complimented. Check the ones you would like to see more of in your marriage. Circle the three most important ones. Start focusing on these areas and saying "thank you" for any and all things your partner does in these areas. Also look for any little things you can compliment. Commit yourself to doing this for one month. Then go back over the list and see what has improved in your marriage. Express appreciation and compliment your spouse on these improvements.

BEHAVIORS OF MARRIED COUPLES

___ Showing affection
___ Exhibiting arguing skills
___ Having a good/bad attitude
___ Keeping commitments
___ Using communication skills
___ Showing consideration
___ Talking things over
___ Expressing creativity
___ Handling financial matters
___ Showing flexibility
___ Developing friendships
___ Exhibiting generosity
___ Enjoying gift-giving
___ Practicing honesty
___ Doing household tasks
___ Rearing children
___ Giving compliments
___ Listening attentively
___ Making love
___ Being patient
___ Being playful
___ Planning romantic activities
___ Expressing a sense of humor
___ Demonstrating sensitivity
___ Showing appreciation

WHY FUN IS CRITICAL TO HAPPY MARRIAGES

When couples first fall in love, one of the major factors that causes the love to flourish is fun. Couples in love have *lots* of fun, both planned and spontaneous. It isn't surprising, then, that couples who have enduring, happy marriages do the same. Conversely, one of the major complaints among troubled couples is that the fun has drained out of the marriage.

Think about this for a moment. What was your courtship like? Did you look forward to being with your lover? Did you feel you could hardly wait to get together? Did the two of you plan lots of outings together to do things you loved? Did you laugh a lot and have a great time? Did you joke around about common everyday things? Were you comfortable being silly with each other?

If these questions evoke positive responses, then you are among the vast majority. Fun is a big part of the early stages of love. In fact, one of the main reasons people fall in love is the way they feel when they are together. How people feel when they are with their spouses also has a major bearing on the happiness and endurance of the marriage.

All of the research into love and happy marriages bears out the fact that there's a direct relationship between love and fun. Couples who have great marriages kid around with each other on a daily basis and plan for fun time on a weekly basis. It would follow, then, that a couple who wants to have a happy and enduring marriage will do the same.

Unfortunately, having fun isn't so easy. Oh, it's easy enough in early love—it flows naturally. But then work, community commitments, household chores, and child-rearing start to take precedence. This is natural. The trouble is, when the fun goes, love also starts to fade. As fun drains out of the relationship, so do the good feelings. And when the good feelings are gone, partners often look for someone else to have fun with.

Having fun, then, is a critical ingredient for a happy marriage. But it doesn't come automatically. It must be planned for and insisted on and must, of course, happen between the partners. Having fun individually with family and friends is great, but it doesn't count toward making love prosper.

Love Potion

Working individually, make a list of the fun things you like to do. Review the things you did together before you got married and write them down. Remember the fun you had when you were a kid and jot down what you did. Include the things you have fantasized trying and fun activities that don't cost any money as well as everyday fun things like hugs, compliments, and jokes.

Once you both have your lists, trade them. In the next month, do three things off your partner's fun list. Enjoy doing some of the fun things your spouse likes to do even if they aren't exactly your types of fun. As an extra, plan to put some fun into your sex life.

One caution. During the fun times, agree to not deal with conflict. Dealing with conflict is necessary in a marriage, but it also ruins fun. So tackle conflict at other times, and lay it aside when you are out having fun.

Chapter 28

Mind Reading 101

Marriage therapists warn of mind reading. Typical mind reading thoughts like, "If he loved me, he would have known what I wanted" or "If he doesn't know why I'm mad, I'm not going to tell him!" are detrimental to a relationship.

When therapists say this, they're really talking about two things. First, when you take action based on what you believe your spouse is thinking, you run the risk of being wrong. And second, if you get angry when your spouse doesn't read your mind and do what you want, then you are likely to be angry a lot. This is the "bad" kind of mind reading.

But, there's a good kind of mind reading too.

Happy couples, in fact, do it on a daily basis. They tend to know their spouses so well that they anticipate their spouses' needs and desires and act to respond to them. For example, one partner knows that the other has had a really hard day, so he arranges a relaxing evening. Or one spouse may say no to an invitation, knowing the other would likely not want to go.

In happy marriages, such mind reading is common. Even if it's off-base, it doesn't do any harm. The person coming home from the hard day may well say, "Yes, it has been a hard day, but you know what? I think I'd love to go out dancing tonight." Or, "Actually, I would like to accept that invitation. Would you mind if I called back and accepted it?"

Also, partners in successful relationships tend to be sensitive to each other's moods. Subtle nonverbal cues alert them when something is wrong. Often these cues will prompt questions like, "You seem preoccupied today. Would you like to talk about what's on your mind?" Or, "You aren't yourself today. What's going on with you?" Such questions are a great comfort to the person being asked; they make him or her feel loved and cared for on a deep level.

In marriages in which mind reading is a problem, partners are frequently incorrect and then base their actions on those false assumptions. Or, partners develop a pattern of interpreting each other's thoughts in a negative light. If this is the case in your relationship, these patterns must be broken. The way to do this is to make a commitment to each other to check before decisions are made and actions taken.

Make a habit of asking questions like, "You seem angry with me. Is that right?" and "It seems to me that you would rather not go to that party. Is that right?" Using questions like these can dramatically improve the way you communicate. Not only do they clear up miscommunication but also the mere asking of the questions shows you care about your spouse.

Love Potion

Practice mind reading with your spouse. Agree to make a game of it for two weeks. Here are the rules: At least once a day read each other's minds and determine how you think your spouse is feeling or what he or she is thinking. Then check it out with questions like, "What I think you are thinking right now is that we should not go out tonight. Is that right?" Or, "What I think you are feeling right now is disappointment. Is that right?" Keep score and decide what the winner gets when the two weeks are up.

Chapter 29

DEEP-SIXING SELF-FULFILLING PROPHECIES

Self-fulfilling prophecies in a marriage are destructive. They result from a process that sets a couple up for the same arguments over and over again. The arguments get worse over time and typically don't end with anything positive for either person. Following is an example of how they get started, how they are perpetuated, and how they undermine the happiness of a marriage.

Let's say a husband asks his wife to bring home his favorite ice cream one evening on her way home from work. She agrees. He reminds her not to forget because he wants to have it when he watches his favorite TV show that night. The wife tells him not to worry, she won't forget. When the husband's show comes on, he goes looking for his ice cream, but it's not there. The husband asks his wife what happened and she apologetically admits that she forgot it. Walking off in a huff, the husband says, "I can't believe you did this to me. You knew how important it was to me. I even reminded you." The wife again apologizes. Still, there's a similar incident a couple of weeks later.

Once the same mistake is made a couple of times, the offended spouse unconsciously decides this is the way it is going to be from now on. But, nice guy that he is, he decides to give his wife another chance. Almost predictably, she blows it.

Both she and her husband expected she would, and she did. When this happens, the foundation is laid for the creation of a self-fulfilling prophecy that can wreak marital havoc.

From now on, the husband assumes his wife isn't responsible enough to keep her commitments. Then he starts to act on this assumption. The next time he wants ice cream, he gets it himself. He also drives across town to pick up his dry cleaning because he needs his blue suit the next day and thinks to himself, "I wish I could get Susan to pick up my suit, but I can't rely on her. She'd probably forget it like usual."

Each time something like this happens, a little more anger builds up.

Then one day the husband makes a remark about needing to have his dress shoes picked up that day at the shoe repair shop. He mutters under his breath that he just doesn't have time to pick them up but that he really needs them for church on Sunday. His wife then asks if he would like her to pick the shoes up. He replies no and says he will do it himself.

Guess what happens next. He forgets. And whom does he blame? His wife, of course. Why? "Because," he says, "my wife is so irresponsible, I can't rely on her to do anything. I have to do everything, and I just can't do it all myself. My wife needs to help, but I can't rely on her for anything!"

In essence she gets blamed for no reason. In fact, she even offered to pick up the shoes and her offer was refused. She points this out to her husband, saying, "I asked you if you wanted me to pick up your shoes, and you said no. How in the world am I to blame for you forgetting to pick up your shoes?"

He replies, "I knew if I asked you, you would forget. You always do. I can't do it all myself. But I can't rely on you either." What a mess!

The good thing is that self-fulfilling prophecies can be laid to rest so that they don't keep harming the relationship. To get rid of them requires consciously identifying and discussing them.

They are easy to identify. If they are a part of your marriage, they will manifest themselves accompanied by blame, anger, and words like, "That's the way you always do it!" and "I knew it. I knew it. That's just the way you are!" Or, "I didn't ask because I knew that's what would happen." When feelings and statements like these are present, a self-fulfilling prophecy is probably at work.

Once the dynamic is identified, all it takes to begin to abolish it is discussion. Self-fulfilling prophecies are some of those devils that cannot stand the light of day. The very act of talking about them destroys them. To do so, though, you may have to wait until neither of you is angry over an incident surrounding the prophecy.

Love Potion

Discuss self-fulfilling prophecies. Ask each other the following questions:

1. Are you aware of any self-fulfilling prophecies that affect our relationship? If so, what are they?
2. What do I do that annoys you on a regular basis?
3. What don't I do that annoys you on a regular basis?
4. What angers you that you don't tell me about?

Take turns asking and answering these questions. The answers should help bring out any devilish self-fulfilling prophecies so they can be destroyed. (Hint: Don't get too serious when asking these questions. Be honest in your answers and nondefensive when you listen to your spouse's answers. And have fun with it. It will be much more curative that way.)

Chapter 30

THE MOST IMPORTANT INVESTMENT YOU CAN MAKE

Time. That's the most important investment you can make in your marriage. Consider this: The average American finds time to watch between two and three hours of television a day but typically spends an average of eighteen minutes a week of quality time with a spouse.

Quality time is defined as time spent together talking attentively, expressing affection physically, discussing things only related to the two of you (parenting issues don't count), looking at each other, having fun, relaxing (television time doesn't count, as it does nothing positive for the relationship), eating quietly together, and spending time worshipping or praying.

Accounting for all of the above, the average length of quality time couples spent together was eighteen minutes a week. This research was conducted by Dr. Paul Pearsall with more than five thousand couples and reported in his book *Super Marital Sex*.

Eighteen minutes a week. That's not much, is it? In fact, I don't know much that you can do for only eighteen minutes a week that will produce a lot of good results. All the other major activities of our life, such as work and taking care of the household and children take up considerable time. We even spend more time doing the laundry and cutting the grass than engaging in quality time with our spouse. Yet one of the most important aspects of our life is our marriage.

Perhaps you are thinking this may be true for other people but not for you. If so, I invite you to take the following test. It's similar to the one that was given to the couples in Dr. Pearsall's research.

THE QUALITY MARITAL TIME TEST

Estimate the average amount of minutes you spend each week in the following activities.

_____ 1. Looking at each other only to admire the other person

_____ 2. Talking about your marriage

_____ 3. Discussing the news

_____ 4. Just being together while one person does something like reading, sewing, or listening to music. Television time doesn't count, as it's more like hypnosis than quality time

_____ 5. Eating alone together

_____ 6. Worshipping, meditating, or praying together

_____ 7. Talking with your spouse about things that concern only the two of you. Don't count time discussing children or in-laws. Also, only count time spent talking with the television off

_____ 8. Hugging, making love, kissing, and touching. Don't count quick hugs and kisses or touching while sleeping

_____ 9. Walking leisurely together. Don't count speed-walking

_____ **Total quality marital minutes**

In the research that was conducted, participants not only couldn't count time watching television, but also had to subtract any time spent watching television from the total quality minutes. The reason for this was because Dr. Pearsall views television as an addiction that robs couples of valuable time that could be spent on intimacy. I leave it up to you to decide whether this is a valid concern in your marriage.

Getting back to the test, how do you feel about the results? Are you happy with the amount of quality time you spend together? Or are you thinking it would be a good idea to increase the amount of quality time you spend with your spouse?

#25 Love Potion

Go out to breakfast or lunch as a couple on the weekend. Take a pad and pencil and the Quality Marital Time Test with you. Each of you should pick the number one area in which you would like to spend more quality time together. Spend ten minutes on each area brainstorming ways you can increase the time spent. Pick one or two ideas from each list and make a commitment to put them into action next week.

ESTABLISHING PRIORITIES (PREFERABLY THE *RIGHT* ONES)

W hether or not a couple takes time to talk about and set priorities, the priorities get set anyway. As married life progresses, choices are made and more time gets allotted to some things than others.

In the United States, if you ask people to list their priorities in rank order, most will list them as:

1. God
2. Family
3. Work
4. Recreation

While this list is common, it's curious for two reasons. First, it doesn't specifically include the marriage. Second, it's rarely the way many people order their lives in reality.

While I don't want to suggest to couples what priorities are *right* to adopt, I would like to stress that marriage should be near the top of the list.

Marriage should come before all other people, events, and activities—even before your children. In fact, the best thing you can do for your children is to put your marriage first. The better the relationship between you and your spouse, the better you will be able to attend to your children's needs. Even work benefits from a happy marriage, since people who are happily married are healthier and miss less work.

Love Potion

Write a love letter to your spouse. In it, say how much you enjoy being with him or her—that he is your top priority, why she is so important to you. List the qualities you admire in him. Get a love stamp and mail the card or put it in her pillowcase so she will find it at bedtime.

Chapter 32

FORGIVENESS FOR HEARTBREAK AND PAIN

Forgiveness is an easy concept to grasp. We are told from the time we are children that we are supposed to apologize if we hurt someone and forgive if someone harms us. Parents teach forgiveness, as does every major religion. You would think with all of this teaching it would be easy to forgive. But it's not.

A lot of variables go into our decision to forgive. It depends on things like:

1. The degree of hurt we feel
2. Whether we assess the act to be premeditated or an accident
3. How many times the person has done the same or similar things
4. How much we love the person
5. How much we depend on the person
6. Our mood at the time
7. How loved we feel at the time
8. The behaviors of forgiveness our parents modeled
9. The degree to which our spiritual faith influences us
10. Whether or not we are willing to continue putting energy into holding a grudge
11. Whether or not the person committing the offense is contrite

12. What we are watching on television or reading at the moment
13. The advice we get from family and friends
14. How stressed we are
15. How often the person has forgiven us

With all of these variables affecting our decision to forgive or not, it's no wonder forgiveness doesn't come easily. But it must, if love is to survive and flourish.

Relationships are dependent on forgiveness. We all make mistakes, sometimes on purpose and sometimes by accident or through sins of omission. There's no way around it. This being the case, every partner in every relationship must learn to give and receive forgiveness.

Love cannot blossom if either person in the relationship is full of anger, rage, or resentment. Rather, love must confront errors, faults, omissions, and hurts—and forgive them all.

Forgiveness isn't an option in marriage. Either it's present in the measure necessary for the survival of the marriage or the relationship will end—emotionally or in divorce court.

What this means is that forgiveness is serious business. Couples with the happiest marriages learn to forgive and forget. Other couples forgive but don't forget. These can still be happy, stable marriages. However, some of the couples in more troubled relationships want forgiveness for themselves but are unwilling to give it to their partners. Other troubled couples hold and feed their grudges.

The goal, then, for couples wishing to build and maintain a happy marriage, is to learn to forgive and forget. If they can't forget, they at least must learn to forgive. While forgiveness isn't always easy, it's always possible. Love Potion Number 27 provides a doorway into forgiveness.

Love Potion

Set aside about an hour to write a letter to your spouse. This letter is for your eyes only. It isn't to be shared with your spouse or anyone else.

Pick an issue you are upset with your spouse about. Start writing everything you think and feel. Don't worry about being reasonable, rational, or logical. Just write whatever comes to mind. Include all of your fears and suspicions.

State in the letter how you wish your spouse would act toward you and how you think he or she should handle the problem. Make sure to write about how you feel—any hurt, shame, betrayal, jealousy, blame, sadness, anger, fear, or resentment. Write about anything you might want to do to get back at your spouse for hurting you.

Once you are satisfied that you have committed all of your negative thoughts and feelings to paper, start a second letter. In this letter, write about the love and compassion you feel for your spouse. Talk about understanding how he or she could have messed up and that you forgive him or her. Write about your spouse's good points and how much you appreciate him or her. If you have any trouble writing the positive letter, think of the kindest, most forgiving person you know and imagine that this person is helping you write the letter.

When you are done writing both letters, burn the first letter (safely, please). Then decide whether or not you want to give your spouse the second letter. If not now, save it in a safe place to give at a later time. Now go treat yourself to something you love to eat or do.

THE MYTH THAT CAN TORPEDO YOUR MARRIAGE

Of the many myths about marriage, one very common one is so destructive it can cause the breakup of marriages. The myth is this: If that wonderful, passionate feeling you had when you married goes away, the love must have gone out of the marriage. This is often expressed between spouses when one says to the other, "I love you, but I'm not 'in love' with you anymore."

What couples are really expressing is a belief that they should always have that loving feeling the marriage started out with. And who can blame them for believing it? It's wonderful to experience the heightened passion of falling in love.

But the myth is dangerous because of the behavior that can result from it. What happens so often is this: When one of the partners concludes that love has died, she is ripe for someone else to come along and fill the void. Very quickly, a new love relationship can form. The passion of this new relationship convinces the person that true love has been found at last. She rushes to end the present marriage and marry the "true love."

I wish it were a requirement of marriage that everyone sign a disclaimer accepting that real love starts where passionate love leaves off. Then I wish a postcard reminding the couple of this fact would be mailed to them every month for two years, starting the thirteenth month of the marriage. This would help get most through the turbulent time when the honeymoon ends, the love blinders come off, and passionate love flies the coop.

Since this is unlikely to happen, please feel free to copy this chapter and give it to the newlyweds you know. Better yet, buy the book for them and put a note in it suggesting they read this chapter first. Remember, the marriage you save may produce the parents of your future grandchildren!

#28 Love Potion

Go to bed half an hour early tonight. Light some candles and put on your favorite music. Snuggle and recall what it was like when the two of you fell in love. Talk of how you felt and of the things you did together. Recall for one another the reasons you wanted to marry the other person. Then let nature take its course.

Chapter 34

KEEPING ROMANCE ALIVE AND HOW TO REKINDLE IT

It's too bad, but romance doesn't happen automatically. It takes commitment and determined effort by both partners. Even in the honeymoon period, a lot of effort goes into being romantic. It may *seem* to happen automatically, but in reality both people put themselves totally into the experience of being loving to each other. They do this, of course, because of how wonderful they feel in the presence of their lover. So, while they're putting a lot of effort into the relationship, it doesn't feel that way because they want to so badly.

Putting this kind of effort into your marriage after the honeymoon stage ends results in a much bigger payoff—mature love. This kind of love is just as wonderful as young love. It's a love that is full of compassion, kindness, appreciation, commitment, forgiveness, and understanding. It even has its periods of extreme passion. Mature love enables you to be happily married for a lifetime.

Love Potion

Take out a sheet of paper and complete the sentence, "I feel loved when you ..." Continue until you have a minimum of thirty-five sentences. Write as fast as you can and complete the sentence with anything that comes to mind. Sometimes your best and most revealing answers will seem to come out of nowhere.

Now finish the sentence, "When we were first in love, I felt loved when you ..." Quickly rewrite and complete the sentence at least fifteen times. Some of your answers may be repeats. That's okay.

Once you have this done, repeat the process with the sentence, "I would like you to show me love by ..." Complete this sentence at least ten times. Use different answers than you did in the first two sentences.

Last, complete the sentence, "I feel romantic when ..." at least ten times.

Now combine your lists, putting a number 1 by the items that are most important to you.

Exchange lists with your spouse. Vow to one another that you will do at least two things per day from your partner's list to show love. Make sure to express your appreciation when your partner follows through.

THE BIGGEST SHOCK IN MARRIAGE

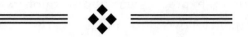

Early in a relationship, we feel totally cared for when we are with our lover. The reason for this is simple. Our cherished one does everything possible to take care of our needs. He or she seems to have an uncanny ability to know just what we desire at any given moment and to fulfill that need. Not since we were young children under the protection of our mothers have we experienced that kind of total fulfillment and caring. It feels so good that we will do anything to keep this wonderful person in our lives (and fulfilling our every need).

Of course, the best way we know to keep this person in our lives is to ferret out their every need and to satisfy it. This in turn causes our loved one to feel deeply cared about, which reinforces their desire to keep fulfilling our needs. What a wonderful cycle!

Too bad it has to end.

At some point in every relationship, one of the partners starts attending to his own needs more than to those of his mate. This happens not by conscious design, but because of human nature. While it feels awesome to have someone attend so closely to our needs, there's no way another person can know and satisfy all of them. To complicate things, at any given moment on any given day, our needs change.

So, a different cycle in the relationship starts. In this new cycle, one person has a need that isn't being met, so he does whatever is necessary to satisfy this need. Because he is focusing on his own need, the spouse is naturally left then to attend to her own needs. This, of course, takes time and attention away from satisfying her partner's needs. Eventually each of the individuals spends more and more time attending to individual needs.

What a shock this is. First you have someone attending to your every whim. Then, almost overnight, you find this person putting his own needs above yours.

In real life, it all happens something like this. During the early stages of the relationship, the couple discusses plans for the weekend. The woman wants to go to the beach and suntan, while the man is dying to go fishing with his friends.

But he remembers the incredible back rub his fiancée gave him the night before, so he lovingly says, "I can't think of anything I would rather do than take you to the beach."

She smiles and replies, "You are so wonderful! But all of your friends are going fishing. Are you sure you wouldn't rather be with them?"

To which he says, "Not a chance! It's the weekend, and I want to be with you, darling."

She then responds, "How very lucky I am to have a great guy like you! But tomorrow you *are* going fishing. I don't want to hear another word about it."

Both then spend the weekend feeling totally at peace and completely cared for.

Fast-forward a couple of years, and the same scenario is played out in a dramatically different way. Let's say the couple is again making weekend plans.

"I would really like to go to the beach and tan on Saturday," she says.

"I hate the beach," he responds. "I'm going fishing, if you don't mind. I mean, you can go to the beach with your sister, can't you?"

"Why can't we ever do something I want to do," she complains.

"It's the weekend," he says. "That's the only time I have to go fishing. Besides, we always do what you want. I never get to do what I want."

This often ends up in a big fight with both partners feeling unloved and uncared for. These feelings in turn cause the couple to focus more intensely on making sure their own needs get met.

Tragically, if focusing on one's own needs becomes the norm, both the husband and wife are at great risk of falling in love with someone else and having an affair. In the new relationship, the love cycle starts over again. Each person becomes intensely wrapped up in satisfying the other's needs, and in so doing they fall deeply in love. Because their spouses are no longer attending to their needs, they divorce them in favor of this new person who does care enough about them to do so.

I'll give you three guesses what happens next.

Couples who stay together and build happy marriages learn at some point that to be happy they must strike a balance between satisfying their own needs and satisfying the needs of their spouse. This isn't an easy realization to come to. Part of us will always believe that if our spouses truly loved us, they would continue to take care of us the way they did initially. When this doesn't happen, it's natural to feel betrayed. If the couple is immature, this feeling of betrayal is hard to overcome and too often leads to divorce.

Even if a legal divorce doesn't take place, an emotional one often does. Partners find ways to avoid intimacy with each other. Consider whether you ever find yourself using any of these activities in excess to avoid intimacy with your spouse: drinking, spending time with friends, watching television, reading, spending time on the computer (especially in chat rooms), working out, shopping, fantasizing, going to bed early, staying up late, camping out on the phone, focusing on hobbies, volunteering, masturbating, complaining, refusing to make love, refusing to talk, going to the movies alone, having sex but not making love, falling asleep on the couch, coming home late, bringing work home from the office, taking drugs, reading every word of the newspaper, or spending too much time with the children.

Please note that I said emotional divorces are made up of doing these things *excessively*. Most of these normal activities are just fine in moderation. But taken to excess they are effective means of ending a marriage without ending it legally. These things allow the partners to avoid being intimate with each other.

By intimacy, I don't mean sexual intimacy (though that can suffer greatly too). The kind of intimacy I am talking about is when two people harmoniously share their lives. A couple able to achieve this kind of intimacy can have an awesome marriage, with both partners' needs being met.

But to arrive at this point, every couple must deal with the shock of discovering their spouses aren't placed on this earth to satisfy their every need. This is a formidable task. The good news is that you can build and maintain a mature and happy marriage in which you meet each other's needs and your own.

Love Potion

Go out for pizza, just the two of you. Get a booth and sit on the same side, as lovers often do. Or, make goo-goo eyes across the table while holding hands. Reminisce about the things you did together when you first fell in love. Ask each other what your favorite things would be to do together (other than making love!). Make plans to act on them as soon as possible.

Chapter 36

ADVANCED FORGIVENESS

One clear difference between couples that succeed and couples that fail is the ability to forgive. In great marriages, couples forgive and forget. In lousy marriages, the couples nurse grudges and plan revenge. Many couples lie somewhere in between these two extremes.

Where a couple falls on this continuum between forgiveness and vengeance depends on the age and maturity of the partners. It's unreasonable to expect young couples to "forgive and forget." The best I think they can hope to achieve is to learn to forgive. Only after years of marriage and lots of practice will a couple come to both forgive *and* forget.

One of the toughest hurdles young couples have to overcome is accepting that both partners are going to make mistakes. Some will be accidental, while others will result from poor judgment. And some will simply be selfish and thoughtless acts.

When you feel your spouse deliberately has done something wrong, it's natural to think, "If my spouse really loved me, he would not have done this to me." It may be difficult to realize that both of you, by virtue of being human, are only trying to satisfy your own needs. Most of what people do in life isn't *to* someone but rather in an effort to satisfy a personal need. And even if the action is done *to* someone else, it's still carried out because of a perceived need. For example, revenge is motivated by a need (albeit dysfunctional) to respond to anger or hurt.

Knowing that all people are motivated primarily by their own needs helps us understand that our spouse's actions are most likely not intended to hurt us, but rather to satisfy a personal need. Focusing on our partner's needs can help us empathize or understand the reasons for those actions. And empathy helps us to forgive.

Still, because forgiving is so difficult, we must have some motivation to do so. Motivation to forgive may be faith based. Most religions teach us to forgive those who offend us. Another motivation is our own need for peace of mind. Since peace of mind and hate cannot coexist, we must either forgive or sacrifice at least a portion of our inner peace.

A third motivation comes from knowing a stable and happy marriage can't exist without forgiveness. Either we learn to forgive or we give up our chances for a happy marriage.

Please realize that you can't avoid the issue of forgiveness by finding another spouse. Even with another partner, learning forgiveness will be a prerequisite to a happy marriage.

Love Potion

This is an advanced exercise in forgiveness. While it's highly worthwhile for couples to do the exercise together, it won't be easy. Don't do it if either of you are tired, feeling irritable, or are at odds with each other. Set a maximum time limit of ninety minutes for this exercise. If you don't finish, which is likely, set a time to complete it on another day.

Before you start, decide how to reward yourselves—such as going out to eat or to a movie—when you are done.

Begin by writing two lists each. On your first list, jot down any things you are angry or resentful about with your spouse. This first list represents the things you need to forgive your spouse for. (Hint: Write them down even if you don't feel like you can—or want to—forgive these things right now.)

On the second list write things you know you've done to anger or upset your spouse. Write only actions he or she is aware of—this isn't meant to be an exercise in confession. Make sure to include things for which you don't feel you deserve forgiveness.

Once your lists are complete, flip a coin to see who goes first. Whoever wins the toss gets to choose one item from their first list followed by one from the other's first list. Discuss each thoroughly and then trade off, discussing an item from each of your second lists. As you listen to each other, abide by the listening rules in chapter 20, "The Rules of Listening."

The purpose of this exercise is to clear the air of both resentment and guilt. The results can be cathartic. Now express affection for each other and go do the fun thing you planned to do before you started this difficult exercise.

Chapter 37

KISS AND TELL: PART 2

I f you asked and answered some of the questions in chapter 17, "Kiss and Tell: Part 1," you are likely looking forward to part 2. Getting to know each other can be a highly positive addiction. The process draws people closely together; even closer than they were during the early days of their love.

Here are the instructions. Change them, if you wish, to suit your purposes and relationship, especially if it will make the process of "Kissing and Telling" more fun.

KISS AND TELL INSTRUCTIONS:

1. Flip a coin to see who goes first. The winner decides whether to Kiss or Tell.
2. The Kisser gives the Teller a kiss (preferably passionate) and picks a question to ask.
3. The Kisser listens, following the Rules of Listening (chapter 20).
4. The Teller answers the question to the best of his or her ability.
5. Switch roles. The new Kisser can choose to ask the same question or a different one.

6. Use your sense of humor. Laughter and all forms of encouragement are strongly suggested.

KISS AND TELL QUESTIONS

1. Which of your senses is the most acute? Which is the least?
2. If you could have the body of a movie star, whose would you pick and why?
3. What are your three fondest memories of us being together?
4. What are the three things you value most about our relationship?
5. Whose marriage do you admire most? Why?
6. Whose marriage do you think is the worst? Why?
7. What does being intimate mean to you?
8. What is the single most important ingredient of a happy marriage?
9. What are four habits you wish you could change? How would you benefit from these changes?
10. What is one thing you would like me to change about myself? Why?
11. What do you feel is the best thing about you? The worst?
12. What do you think is your most important contribution to our relationship?

Love Potion

Cook a gourmet meal together on a Saturday evening. During the week, plan everything from the menu to the music and the table centerpiece. Either arrange for the children to be out of the house or plan to eat after the children are in bed. Eat by candlelight and enjoy!

ESTABLISH YOUR OWN TRADITIONS

Traditions are ways in which we celebrate life's significant events on a repeated basis. In short, they are celebrations. Some traditions are big, some small. They can denote anything from the unique way we greet each other to the way we celebrate a major holiday or a birthday.

Early in marriage, couples associate traditions with the ones that existed in their families. Quite naturally, each partner is attached to doing things the way they were done in his or her childhood. But in order for a marriage to thrive, partners must establish their own rituals.

Considering all the traditions you grew up with, this may seem to be an almost insurmountable task. It isn't, though. It takes both partners' willingness to let go of the way their parents did things, even if it seems perfectly reasonable to follow their example. Why? Because it's critical for couples to break their bonds with their parents. It's the first task of marriage (see chapter 14, "The Essential Tasks of Building a Good Marriage").

Before I go on, I have one caveat: Religious traditions are important, and you may want to continue ones you grew up with in the manner dictated by your faith.

The good news is that it can be a lot of fun establishing your own way of celebrating. It takes creativity and effort, but the work pays off in traditions that will endear you to each other and that your children will come to look forward to. These new traditions will be what make your family unique.

The smaller traditions most often "just happen." No one really plans them; rather, they evolve naturally. For example, my wife and I poke each other whenever one of us says something the other disagrees with. How this started is a mystery to me, but it provides us with a lot of laughs.

We've also established a tradition of coming home and spending ten minutes or so in our bedroom unwinding and talking about our day. Another is our rule for making the bed: The last one out has to do it. (We've had a lot of fun with this, but the winner often cheats and makes the bed while the loser is in the shower.) Simple and silly things like this are the glue that holds relationships together.

Here are some suggestions for small traditions you could begin. Attach personal touches to make them unique.

1. Going to bed: Spoon, say something special, take turns praying, read to each other.

2. Getting up: Take turns selecting and playing music, give a morning back scratch or massage, exercise together.

3. Leaving in the morning: Share plans for the day, predict positive results, remind each other of a positive trait each of you has, kiss passionately.

4. Connecting during the day: Meet for lunch on Tuesdays, send flowers, put love notes where each will find them throughout the day, call to say "I love you," e-mail a love note.

5. Coming home: Establish a sanctuary where you can meet undisturbed for a few minutes to unwind and

share the day's events, have a glass of wine or a soft drink together, go for a walk.

6. Suppertime: Designate certain nights each week as a pizza or hamburger night, eat-out night, TV tray night, or fast-food night; pick a night when one cooks the other's favorite meal; do the dishes together with your favorite music on.

7. Evenings: Give back rubs on Tuesday, take an early bedroom retreat on Wednesdays to read or do what comes naturally, watch your favorite TV show together, take turns providing a special snack during your favorite show, have a board-game night.

8. Weekends: Take turns planning something special to do, make breakfast for each other, do errands together, have brunch while you are out, try a different restaurant every weekend.

There's no end to the variety of things you can turn into your own traditions. The same is true for the major holidays. These take more effort because of the emotional attachment people have to the traditions they grew up with. However, given time, patience, and understanding, traditions can be tailor-made or adapted for your family.

One good way to start is by talking with each of your in-laws about how they started their traditions. In so doing, you will get great information, and you will likely feel a bit freer to create your own special ways to celebrate the holidays. After all, your parents did!

Love Potion

When you come home from work, ask your spouse to play the FNW (Feel, Need, Want) game with you. In this game you each take turns completing the following sentences out loud: "I feel …," "I need …," and "I want…." For example, "I feel tired," "I need to sit down and rest," and "I want to take the phone off the hook while I rest." Mirror the sentences back to your mate: "What I hear you saying is that you feel tired, you would like to rest, and you want the phone off the hook. Is that right?" Once in a while, for the fun of it, see if you can read each other's minds.

TAMING THE MONEY MONSTER: PART 1

A couple's ability to handle financial matters is one of the variables that determines the stability and happiness of the marriage. In great marriages, couples learn how to handle money matters together and to spend less than they make. The more trouble couples have doing this, the less stable and happy the marriage is.

Money issues take time and effort to master. For most couples it may take years to learn to work together on finances. It helps to be patient with each other, learning in the meantime as much as you can to help get your finances under control.

To start the journey toward money mastery, it's important for partners to understand each other's views on it. To help you do this, here are some sentence completions for each of you to answer verbally or in writing. If you wish, you can give several endings to each answer, but each answer should relate to money.

1. I think money is …
2. As a child, my family was …
3. I think you think money is …
4. When we fight about money, I wish you would …
5. We disagree about money because …
6. We would get along better about money if I would …

7. When we fight about money I know you are only trying to ...
8. We could have more money if ...
9. My parents always told me ...
10. I have had my worst problems with money when ...
11. I have had my best success with money when ...
12. If you really knew me you would know that ...
13. We would not have any problems with money if ...
14. What I know about financial matters I learned ...
15. In the long run, I think ...
16. In the short term, I think we should ...
17. The thing I like about the way we deal with money is ...
18. My greatest fear about money is ...
19. In order to improve our marriage I would be willing to ...
20. I am optimistic about our financial situation because ...

Once you've each taken a turn answering these questions, go for a walk and talk about what you learned from each other. Complete the following sentence: "I was surprised to know ..." Discuss the decisions you want to make in light of this information.

Love Potion

How long has it been since you went on a honeymoon? Plan an evening of soft music and candles. Talk about where you would like to go on a second honeymoon. Set a date to go. Follow up by getting travel brochures, finding out what the costs are, and putting together a plan to finance it.

Chapter 40

TAMING THE MONEY MONSTER: PART 2

Following are three commonly suggested steps for couples to take to gain control of their finances. They require some work, but will be enormously helpful if both of you are willing to participate. Even couples with no financial problems may want to do them because of the potential insights that can be gained.

The first step takes a major commitment and is tough to do. The other two are a lot of fun. Put the three steps together and what you get is a whole lot more control over your finances. Plus, you will likely greatly improve your chances of being happily married for a lifetime!

Step 1: Write down every cent you spend every day for a month. Every cent. No matter what you spend the money on, write it down. Also, save all your receipts and make notes on them so at the end of the month you'll be able to remember what the receipts were for. To make record-keeping easier, place a small notebook in your car, briefcase, or purse so you can write down expenditures as they occur. Use an envelope to stash your receipts so you don't lose them before month end.

This step isn't so you can prepare a budget, although I suppose you could use the information for that purpose. Rather, you are doing this to give yourselves some knowledge and insight into your spending habits. Most couples have no idea where their money goes or in what quantities. For example, do you know how much you spent on eating out last month? How about on incidentals? If you already know the answers to these questions then you most likely already have the information this activity will yield. If not, then this step is essential for you.

Just thinking about writing down everything you spend will likely bring up some fears or other negative emotions. Talk with each other about your fears and any resistance you have to completing this activity.

When the month is up, take a sheet of legal paper and turn it horizontally, writing across the top the different categories in which you spent your money. Use specific categories: break "entertainment" down into "movies," "restaurants," and "movie rentals." If you are familiar with a computer spreadsheet program, you may want to enter the information into your computer. Enter all of what you spent and total the columns.

Now discuss the results (please note: Money issues are very touchy and can make people fearful and defensive. So, be kind and gentle with each other as you have your discussion). Ask yourselves these questions.

1. Which categories surprise or even shock you? Why?
2. Do you feel like you got your money's worth in each category?
3. In which categories do you think you overspent?
4. In which categories do you want to cut expenses?
5. How can you spend less?

Step 2: Write and complete fifty endings to the following sentence: "I will be satisfied when I have enough money to ..." Now make a list of the things you feel you need to be happy in the present. Discuss your lists with your spouse and set some financial goals. Write them down and put them where you can see them on a daily basis.

Step 3: List ways you can enjoy life and satisfy your needs without spending money. Brainstorm and write down every kind of pleasure you can enjoy without spending money. Whenever you have an urge to spend money on something from one of the categories in which you tend to overspend, see if you can substitute something from your list of free pleasures.

Love Potion
#35

Save some money to treat your spouse. Write a love note to your spouse saying that the enclosed money you saved is for spending on himself or herself. Put it somewhere your spouse will be surprised to find it. Get ready for a big kiss and hug!

Chapter 41

THE CONSCIOUS LOVE REVIVAL

S pend a moment reminiscing about when you first fell in love with your spouse. Do you remember how you greeted each other? How about the way you said good-bye? Like most couples, your hellos and good-byes were likely punctuated with a passionate embrace and kiss. You communicated your feelings through the physical acts of loving and kissing. And wasn't it an awesome feeling? Not only did it make you feel loved, but it most likely made you feel incredibly connected to this person.

Compare this to the way you greet your spouse now. Do you, like so many couples, peck each other on the cheek? How about after a long day apart? Do you still enthusiastically communicate your love through a passionate hug and kiss? There's a good chance if you have been married for more than two years that the answer is no.

Couples often wonder why they have drifted apart, why they don't have any passion left for each other. One common reason is that they've stopped treating each other as they did when they were first in love. They don't consciously stop doing these things; life just seems to take over and push them aside one by one. Unfortunately, though, when the actions of love cease, the communication of love is dramatically reduced.

The good news is that you can get the passion back in your marriage if you start replicating the behaviors of your early relationship. As you bring back these loving actions, the passion will return as well.

Most couples want to feel love before they act lovingly. They think if you don't "feel it," then behaving in a loving fashion is fake. This is understandable. Loving actions come naturally to couples when they are first in love, but this condition doesn't last. It might be nice if it did, but it doesn't.

If love is to survive, the couple must realize that it flourishes over the long term when partners consciously treat each other in loving ways. That is, they make decisions daily to do things that will make their spouse feel loved. When the couple starts to do this, the relationship evolves into a deeper, more mature love.

One of the best ways I know of rekindling love is for partners to recall the ways they communicated their love to each other in the early stages of their relationship. To facilitate this process, pick a time and place to relax and listen to your favorite music from when you were first in love (music greatly enhances memory). If possible, re-create the sights and smells of this time. The idea is to do whatever you can to recapture the memories of how you best expressed your love to each other in the early days.

While re-creating this time, recall for each other the things you both did that made you feel so loved. Take turns completing this sentence: "I felt so very loved when you ..." In so doing, not only will the memories come back but you may well bring your lost feelings of passion to the surface. During the weeks (and years) to follow, surprise your spouse occasionally with one of the things you used to do that made him or her feel so loved in the early days.

The rule to remember here is that "feelings follow actions." If you wait until you feel love to act lovingly, then you probably won't act lovingly very often. The remedy is to act as if you feel all of the love you want, and then your feelings of love will return for real.

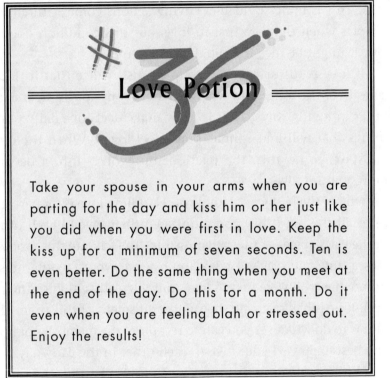

#36 — Love Potion —

Take your spouse in your arms when you are parting for the day and kiss him or her just like you did when you were first in love. Keep the kiss up for a minimum of seven seconds. Ten is even better. Do the same thing when you meet at the end of the day. Do this for a month. Do it even when you are feeling blah or stressed out. Enjoy the results!

Chapter 42

THE SECRET OF WHY WE FALL (AND STAY) IN LOVE

It's important to know why your spouse fell in love with you. If you have this knowledge, you can use it to help your partner stay in love with you. Every spouse needs to help her partner maintain that ardor. Love isn't one-sided. To be loved, we must act in loving ways.

So here is the secret why your spouse fell in love with you: It resulted from the way he or she felt about himself or herself in your presence. For women, it's like this: You fell in love with your husband because he said and did things that made you feel you were capable, appreciated, respected, intelligent, sexy, and beautiful. For men, you fell in love with your wife because she said and did things that made you feel capable, appreciated, respected, intelligent, sexy, and handsome.

Couples who have been happily married for a lifetime report that their spouses continue to make them feel this way. Love is dependent on the partners saying and doing things to make their spouses feel good about themselves.

Now, I strongly feel each individual in a relationship is totally responsible for his or her own happiness and self-esteem. Relying on another person for your happiness and feelings of self-worth isn't a functional or healthy way to live. Rather, it's a sure way to end up unhappy and suffering from low self-esteem.

So I assert strongly that individuals must take total responsibility for themselves in these areas.

However, love *is* dependent on how we make the other person feel. There's no way of getting around this. The better partners make their loved ones feel, the better the chance for love to exist. For love to flourish and endure, partners must continue to make each other feel good. If not, love will fade.

Some people respond to this equation negatively. They say, "But I don't want to be responsible for my spouse's psychological well-being." To those who hold this view I respond with, "You only have to do this if you want to be happily married for a lifetime." While it isn't fair for us to put the onus on our spouses to make us happy, it's critical to our relationships that we make our spouses feel special in every way possible.

The more you say and do to make your spouse feel capable, appreciated, respected, intelligent, sexy, and attractive, the more your spouse will respond similarly. This is a fact of life. Loving behavior is responded to most often with loving behavior.

There are some caveats here, though. You cannot anticipate any reward or reciprocation for your loving actions. And you need to be consistent and patient in demonstrating love.

In short:

1. Make your spouse feel capable, appreciated, respected, intelligent, sexy, and attractive.
2. Give your love freely without expectation of reward or reciprocation.
3. Be patient and consistent in saying and doing things to help make your spouse feel good about himself or herself.
4. Your spouse will then feel loved.

5. Your spouse will start to act in ways that will make you feel capable, appreciated, respected, intelligent, sexy, and attractive.

These are the ways partners in long-lasting, happy marriages act with each other. Couples that divorce do the opposite. Though those partners at first said and did things to make each other feel good, at some point they started to say and do things that made each other feel incapable, unappreciated, disrespected, stupid, unsexy, and unattractive.

For a marriage to survive the turbulent times when passionate love wanes, at least one person in the relationship must keep love alive by continuing to make the other person feel good about himself or herself. Of course, it's better if both continue to do so. But, if not, then at least one must take the lead in order to keep the marriage together until the other responds. Too often, though, the one that takes the lead to cheer her partner on loses patience, gets resentful, and gives up. The marriage then comes to an end.

But if you can hold on, the formula will work. Psychologically supporting your spouse will eventually bolster him or her, and your spouse will start to respond in kind. How long will this take? For many it may take between a month and a year. For others it may take several years. But, as my daddy used to say, "Honest effort is never lost." The same applies here: "Love is never lost." It will always come back to you in some fashion or other.

Love Potion

Designate one night a week to not watch television. Make this a date night. Take turns each
week planning what you will do on your date.
Make some nights romantic, some relaxing, and
some just plain fun.

Chapter 43

HOW LIFE AFFECTS SEXUAL INTIMACY

W hen couples first get married, living is normally easy. Stressful circumstances are for the most part foreign to most couples during the early years and before children. Even careers are typically pretty tame in terms of producing stress.

Times without stress, however, don't last. Life, as it progresses, produces all kinds of stress. Much of it just seems to creep up on us. Often we are so unaware of it that when asked if we are stressed, we honestly reply with something like, "Stressed out? Me? No way. I don't have much stress in my life at all." But the reality may be the exact opposite without us recognizing it.

When the flames of stress start to lick at our heels, our sex life also gets singed. Here is the formula to remember: The more stress in your life, the less sexual satisfaction. When couples reach a point where one or both is burdened with career and family problems, they often stop having sex altogether. Or, at least, their sex life slows to such infrequency that the couple can't remember the last time they made love.

Go over the following list of common stress producers with your spouse and give each a ranking of zero to ten depending on how true you think the statement is for you as a couple. A rank of ten would mean this area in your lives is producing a lot of stress. Zero means no stress is coming from this area whatsoever.

The Stress Test

_____ 1. One or both of us are experiencing stress at work.

_____ 2. One or both of us are at odds with our parents or in-laws.

_____ 3. We simply don't have enough time to do every-thing we must do.

_____ 4. We have financial problems.

_____ 5. We don't have time for recreation.

_____ 6. Our children take most of our free time and attention.

_____ 7. Recently one or both of us experienced a major loss.

_____ 8. We spend little time with friends.

_____ 9. One or both of us have little opportunity to be by ourselves.

_____ 10. We recently moved and now live more than fifty miles from family and friends.

_____ 11. One or both of us have to tend to our elderly parent's needs.

_____ 12. One or both of us have had an affair in the last two years.

_____ 13. One or both of us drink more than three drinks a day or get high one or more times per week.

_____ 14. We don't express love, appreciation, and respect to and for each other on a daily basis.

_____ 15. One or both of us are in a life transition.

_____ 16. One or both of us have significant health problems.

_____ 17. One or both of us are having problems with depression or another emotional problem.

_____ 18. One or both of us take mood-altering drugs (prescribed or illicit).

_____ **Total**

Once you have totaled the score, come to a consensus on how satisfied you are as a couple with your sex life. Don't base your answer on how many times you have heard it's "normal" to make love per week. Rather, base it on how satisfied you feel emotionally about your sex life. Give it a rating from one to ten. If you cannot agree on the number, each of you can score it from one to ten and then average the two scores.

There are a couple of ways to assess the results of the stress test. First, if you score your satisfaction level to be seven or above, then stress isn't much of a factor in your sex life. This is good. But you may want to retake this test at a more stressful time in your future.

If the two of you score your level of satisfaction less than seven and if your total score is more than sixty, then stress is likely taking a toll on your sex life. It's also possible that you may have a low total; however, if you scored any of the questions above seven, then stress may also be affecting your sex life.

To improve your sex life, you can try to reduce the stress, change the way you respond to the stressor(s), or find ways to increase sexual satisfaction despite stress. Different ways to address stress are discussed in later chapters on sex.

#38
Love Potion

The next time your spouse is experiencing emotional pain, listen carefully to his or her story. Get every detail and then give all the sympathy you can. We all need understanding and sympathy at some time or another. We also need to know we aren't alone in our suffering, that someone cares for us so deeply that he or she will help shield us from the harshness of the world. Remember to give sympathy often. It's an unconditional gift of love, and it will serve to fuel your relationship so it can reach great heights.

Chapter 44

THE FRIENDS AND FOES OF SEX

L ife is difficult," says Scott Peck in his book *The Road Less Traveled*. So is sex. Why? Well, because life is difficult.

The very act of daily living interferes with sex. This is why sex comes so easily to young lovers. Not only is it still erotic when a person is young, but life is so simple that it doesn't intrude into the bedroom. Truth be known, young lovers don't come out of the bedroom often enough to let life interfere!

In the last chapter, three ways were offered for dealing with stress that encroaches on your sex life. These include reducing the stress, changing the way in which you respond to the stressor(s), and finding ways to increase sexual satisfaction despite the stress.

There's much written about how to "turn on" your spouse, but in my estimation, most couples already know how to do this. I'm not saying that it's not good to learn about and explore new and different ways to please each other, because these are good things to do. I am saying, though, that as long as stress is intruding into the bedroom, sex will likely be lackluster, infrequent, and unsatisfying.

Fortunately, some relatively easy things can help mitigate immediately the adverse affects of stress on your sex life. Here are a few you might consider:

- Go to bed earlier. Stress is much easier to deal with if both partners are well rested. Also, fatigue zaps sexual desire.
- Put a lock on the bedroom door if you have children. This will reduce the stress that comes from fear that a child may walk in at the wrong moment.
- Take a short trip, even if it's just for the weekend, and go somewhere alone. Sex thrives away from home.
- Establish a pattern of listening and showing each other empathy. Not only do listening and empathy lower stress levels but they also increase feelings of love and passion.
- Take a course on stress or buy a good book on the subject. If you keep on dealing with stress the same way you've always dealt with stress, you will likely continue to reap the consequences.
- Go to a large bookstore. Find the section on relationships and pick out a good book on sex. Go home, put on some romantic music, and read the book to each other. Do what the book says.
- Put just as much effort into being loving after sex that you put into being loving before sex. This will bolster your confidence to go out and handle the stress at hand. It will also reinforce sexual desire.

All of these things together and separately can help couples recover the satisfaction they once had in the early days of their love. If they don't help, several possibilities need to be examined. Ask yourselves these questions:

- Is one area of stress overwhelming you? If the stress is short term, then put your sex life on hold, be patient, and wait for the stress to pass. If the stress is ongoing, you will need to find a way to change your circumstances or figure out how to handle stress differently.

- How is your relationship? One of the great foes of good sex is a lousy relationship. If each partner doesn't feel capable, appreciated, respected, intelligent, sexy, and attractive, then sexual satisfaction will diminish markedly. Fix the relationship and sexual satisfaction will return.

- Do you have any physical problems? Medical conditions often affect sexual desire and function. If one or both of you are having health problems, talk with your physician about it. There may well be a simple cure. Also, consider making an appointment with a clinic that specializes in sexuality. Most large cities have them, with all the most up-to-date methods to both diagnose and treat your problem.

Like other areas of marriage, sex is one that must be attended to and worked on. Thinking that sex should always be the way it was in the beginning of your relationship is counterproductive. This attitude never leads to more sexual satisfaction. Rather, it can lead to affairs and divorce.

Couples that stay happily married for a lifetime do what it takes to build and maintain a sex life that satisfies the needs of both partners. You can too. One thing is clear, though: A satisfying sex life takes lots of work and patience. And like so many other areas of marriage, the levels of satisfaction can vary dramatically depending on how much "life" is intruding into the bedroom.

Love Potion

Plan an hour of lovemaking. Play your favorite music and burn incense or candles. Take turns giving each other pleasure at ten-minute intervals. When it's the receiver's turn, this person's only responsibility is to enjoy and give feedback; he or she isn't to give pleasure. After ten minutes, switch roles. Do this back and forth until each of you have had three turns at both giving and receiving. (Hint: If one or both of you reach an orgasm, relax for a few minutes and then go back to it.)

Chapter 45

PUTTING THE SPARKLE
BACK INTO SEX

If you have been married for more than two years, then the
automatic sparkle that comes with young love is likely to
have worn off. As a shiny new car eventually loses its sparkle, so
do marital relationships.

During the early days of marriage, the lovers go kind of "gaga"
upon seeing each other. Adrenaline courses through their veins,
heartbeats quicken, blood pressures rise, and loving feelings swell.
Each person feels intensely alert and hypersensitive to the other's
touch and smell. Every sense, every part of the body responds.
What they're feeling is what we call "love." There's nothing like it!

And in the bedroom, WOW! Sensitivity for each other
reaches a crescendo. The intensity of love reaches its peak.
Physical passion when added to the emotional feeling of love
makes a powerful elixir. It's the stuff that forms the basis for relationships to grow.

While it would seem wonderful for a couple to continue to
live in this state of bliss, it isn't meant to be. The routines of
daily living, familiarity, and predictability take their toll. As time
goes on, not by design or choice, when couples see each other
their heartbeats no longer accelerate, their blood pressures don't
rise, and feelings of love don't swell. In time, as well, body
responses normalize and the "wow" goes away.

But, on a positive note, love between the partners has taken root and been fertilized by passion. Once this happens, the seeds have been sown for the growth of a more permanent, stable, and mature love. This is necessary if a couple is to be happily married for a lifetime. But it's also necessary once in a while to do what it takes to rekindle the passion of early love.

It's necessary for two reasons. The first is because the automatic passion of early marriage always fades and has no ability to regenerate itself. If passion is to survive in a marriage, the partners consciously will have to do what is necessary to keep it. Second, keeping the excitement in your sex life is necessary because love wanes if you don't. Sex is a powerful bonding agent. To not pay attention to it is to let one of the central fetters of marriage shrivel and fade away from neglect.

One of the most destructive marriage myths is that if passion fades then love has been lost. The conclusion that follows is what makes the myth so damaging to the marriage: "I no longer feel passion for my spouse so I need to go find someone else to love." Once this conclusion is drawn, a person is ripe to fall into the trap of a heated affair, during which he further concludes, "I was right. I again feel passionate love, so I should get a divorce and marry my true love." This faulty thinking causes many of the one million annual U.S. divorces.

Here are several suggestions that will help you put the spark back in your marriage.

- Buy a book or take a course in massage together. Practice on each other frequently. Touching and giving are two things that stir the coals of passion.
- Go to bed, turn out the lights, and ask your partner what things he or she absolutely likes best when making love. Take turns putting them into action.

- Ask your partner to name five things that turn him or her on. Make note of and practice them.
- Go to the bookstore and look at books on sex. Pick out one or two. Study the contents together, in bed with your spouse.
- Brainstorm together how you can involve all five senses in your lovemaking.
- Ask your mate what his or her idea of the perfect romantic evening is. Make it a reality.
- Kiss your spouse passionately in the morning. Call to say "I love you" during the day, kiss your spouse passionately when you see each other in the evening, and verbalize your desire to make love that night.

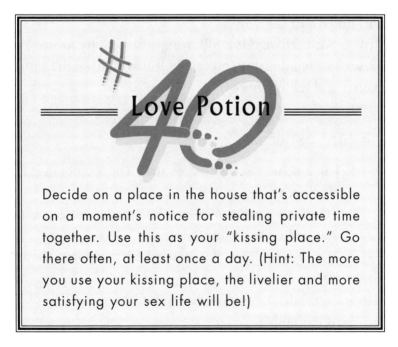

Love Potion #40

Decide on a place in the house that's accessible on a moment's notice for stealing private time together. Use this as your "kissing place." Go there often, at least once a day. (Hint: The more you use your kissing place, the livelier and more satisfying your sex life will be!)

Chapter 46

KISS AND TELL: PART 3

E njoy this third set of questions designed to help you and your spouse get to know each other on a more personal and intimate level. There are few better things you can do to strengthen your love than spending time getting to know each other's innermost thoughts.

If you wish, change the following instructions to suit your purposes and relationship, especially if it will make the process of kissing and telling more fun.

KISS AND TELL INSTRUCTIONS:

1. Flip a coin to see who goes first. The winner decides whether to Kiss or Tell first.
2. The Kisser gives the Teller a kiss (preferably passionate) and picks a question to ask.
3. The Kisser follows the Rules of Listening (see chapter 20).
4. The Teller answers all the questions to the best of his or her ability.
5. Switch roles. The new Kisser can choose to ask the same question or a different one.

6. Use your sense of humor. Laughter and all forms of encouragement are strongly suggested.

KISS AND TELL QUESTIONS: PART 3

1. Are you open to taking risks? If so, what kinds, and what is the biggest chance you have ever taken?
2. Remember a time when I was very upset. How did you feel when I was so upset?
3. Are you open to learning more about sex? If so, what do you think we could do to learn some new things?
4. What is one thing you think we could do to improve our sex life?
5. What would you do if you won a million dollars?
6. What do you like about your job? Dislike?
7. How long do you think you will keep your present job?
8. If you could do anything, what would it be?
9. What are the best three things about having sex with me?
10. What is the most eccentric thing about you? About me?
11. What do you want to do when you retire? At what age do you want to retire?
12. Where would you want to live when you retire?

#41

Love Potion

Starting tonight, every time you get up from watching television, make sure you ask your spouse if you can get him or her anything. Make a habit of doing it without exception. It doesn't matter if the answer is always no. Just by asking you will be communicating your love.

Chapter 47

Do You Feel Bad?

Most people tend to find positive emotions easy to identify and express. Negative emotions are another matter. Many people have trouble identifying them, and some will go out of their way to avoid expressing them.

There's a good reason for this. Negative feelings often provoke negative reactions. If you have experienced negative reactions when you have expressed negative feelings, you may be reluctant to express them in the future.

In addition, you may not have had an adequate role model for expressing negative emotions. The result is that not only do you not know how to express them, but you also have no idea how to identify and name these feelings.

Correcting this situation takes motivation, information, and practice.

If you don't learn to tell your partner how you are feeling, the feelings will either come out "sideways" or pile up until they erupt in an angry outburst. An example of coming out "sideways" is when a person is angry about something and, instead of expressing the anger verbally, refuses to do something the other person wants. Another phrase for this is "passive-aggressive behavior." Anger expressed in such a way seriously undermines a marriage.

Controlling negative emotions, or "keeping them in," also has a damaging effect on a marriage. It takes additional energy to hold these emotions in, and the more negative emotions that are "stuffed," the more energy it takes to hold them in. This robs a person of energy she could use for productive purposes. Also, anger turned inward often becomes depression or takes a toll on the person's physical health.

Ultimately, the risk in stuffing feelings is that you can only hold in so much. When you reach your limit, the slightest thing can cause all of the negative emotions to flood out. If this happens, watch out! Not only do your emotions come out, but they also get expressed with all the energy that's built up.

An example: A husband forgets to take out the garbage and the wife responds with outrage that's out of proportion to the offense. The sheer force of her anger blows him away, and she won't (or can't) hear anything he has to say, not even an apology.

Understanding these dynamics will help to motivate you to express your emotions as they come up, but for you to express them will still take some knowledge and practice.

Here is a list of negative emotions. The next time you are feeling "bad" but can't quite put your finger on the specific emotion, refer to this list to help you identify it.

NEGATIVE FEELING LIST

Abandoned	Anxious	Cowardly
Afraid	Blamed	Depressed
Angry	Bored	Devalued
Animosity	Cheated	Disappointed
Annoyed	Cold	Disapproved of

Discouraged	Helpless	Ostracized
Disgusted	Hopeless	Rejected
Distant	Humiliated	Remorseful
Distrustful	Hurt	Repulsed
Dominated	Ignored	Sad
Embarrassed	Inadequate	Shameful
Enraged	Indifferent	Smothered
Excluded	Insecure	Sorrowful
Fearful	Invisible	Suppressed
Guilty	Lonely	Trapped
Gutless	Mocked	Uneasy
Hate	Nervous	Withdrawn

Identifying your feelings is essential to being able to express them. But even when you have a feeling pegged, it can be difficult to verbalize it to your spouse. This is especially true if your feeling is a result of something he or she said or did. When this is the case, people often fear that rejection or conflict will result if they share their feelings. Still, to avoid the potential destruction that can result from holding feelings back, it's necessary to take the risk of expressing them.

Here is a good way to practice. Working privately, sit down with a pad of paper and pen. Think of at least three circumstances that cause you to feel bad. Refer to the Negative Feeling List and identify what you feel. Then, using the FNW formula write down what you feel, what you need, and what you want. An example would be: "I *feel* ignored when you read the paper at breakfast. I *need* your attention. I *want* you to talk to me at breakfast and not read the paper." Write down at least three of these statements.

When you feel comfortable, take a risk and share one of your statements with your spouse. (Hint: Choose something fairly innocuous and do it at a time when emotions aren't running high.) Have some patience with yourself. The first few times you may make some mistakes. Keep at it, though, and you will become an expert at verbalizing both your feelings and your needs.

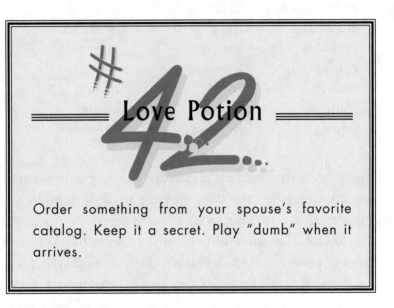

#42

Love Potion

Order something from your spouse's favorite catalog. Keep it a secret. Play "dumb" when it arrives.

Chapter 48

ARE YOU FEELING GOOD?

D o you feel good a lot of the time? Does your spouse say and do things that make you feel capable, appreciated, respected, intelligent, sexy, and attractive? If so, are you good at expressing your appreciation and giving positive feedback?

Sometimes, partners take their spouses' giving behaviors for granted. When confronted, unaware of their sins of omission, they say something like, "My spouse already knows how much I appreciate everything he or she does. There's no need to keep saying thank you."

Wrong! Behavior that goes unappreciated diminishes. One of the most common complaints in marriages is lack of appreciation. The odd thing is that while we human beings have a need to be appreciated for our contributions, we tend to be lackadaisical in our efforts to give the very thing we so badly want given to us.

In longstanding, happy marriages, appreciation is expressed on a regular if not daily basis by both partners. Here is a way to sincerely express your appreciation that is sure to communicate to your spouse:

Use the FNW formula. Pick out something your mate does that really makes you feel good, decide what need it fills, and identify what you want. For instance: "When you come home and kiss me, I *feel* loved. I *need* to feel loved by you, and I *want* you to kiss me every day." Or, "I *feel* grateful when you take time to listen to my problems about work. I *need* to have someone to talk to about what I'm going through. I *want* you to keep listening to me. It makes a big difference to me."

Here is a list of positive feelings to refer to. It can help you express exactly how you are feeling to your spouse.

The Positive Feeling List

Affectionate	Ecstatic	Peaceful
Appreciated	Elated	Playful
Attractive	Encouraged	Pleased
Bold	Energetic	Proud
Brave	Enthusiastic	Reassured
Calm	Excited	Refreshed
Capable	Exhilarated	Resolute
Carefree	Fascinated	Respected
Certain	Festive	Respectful
Cheerful	Frisky	Sexy
Comfortable	Happy	Silly
Confident	Independent	Spirited
Courageous	Inspired	Strong
Creative	Intelligent	Surprised
Curious	Jubilant	Thankful
Debonair	Lighthearted	Tickled
Determined	Lively	Tranquil
Earnest	Loving	Turned on

Love Potion

Write your spouse a love note. Put it in a book he or she is reading.

Chapter 49

WHAT DOES YOUR SPOUSE EXPECT OF YOU?

When two people get married, they have expectations of each other. Yet neither is typically aware of their expectations or the expectations of their partner. As my daddy used to say, "This is a fine kettle of fish." What he meant was that this set of circumstances is a mess, and it's going to be difficult to clean up.

In long-term, happy marriages, partners sort through and come to know each other's expectations. As they become aware of them, negotiations take place and expectations are modified. This process, as you might imagine, takes years, lots of patience, flexibility, understanding, and even some forgiveness.

Rather than hope time will eventually reveal each other's expectations, it's wise to take a more proactive approach. Consciously identifying and communicating them can save a lot of hurt feelings and can help both partners get their needs met.

To help you become more conscious of your expectations, here are questions for you to ask each other.

EXPECTATION EXPLORATION QUESTIONS

Instructions: Use the Rules of Listening found in chapter 20. If you feel one of your spouse's expectations is unreasonable or you are unwilling to meet it, hold back your response until you ask questions and fully understand where your spouse is coming from and why.

After doing this, in a compassionate (and non-defensive way) let your spouse know of your objection. Help your partner discover what need might be motivating this expectation. Then, brainstorm and negotiate other mutually acceptable ways for the need to be met.

Take turns asking and answering each question. Spend time doing this exercise. You may even want to revisit it on several occasions.

1. What are your expectations regarding children? How many do you want? Will we both work or will one stay home to care for the children? If so, for how long?

2. Whose career comes first? Will we both work, or only one of us?

3. How should we handle money? Who will pay the bills? Who will balance the checkbook? How will we decide on long-term investments?

4. How often do you expect we will have sex? Who should initiate it? Are there any taboos?

5. What are your expectations regarding friends? Is it okay to spend time alone with friends? If so, how much time and doing what kinds of things?

6. What are your views on divorce? Do you think it's possible that we might one day divorce? What kinds of things do you think could cause us to divorce?

7. What are your views on monogamy? Do you think it's okay to have an "open marriage"? Why or why not?

8. How do you think we should handle problems that come up? What should we do if one of us becomes extremely angry with the other?

9. What are your views on forgiveness? In marriage, are there any behaviors you feel are totally unforgivable?

10. What expectations do you have for our family in regard to religion and spirituality? What faith-based practices are important to you? How do you view a parent's role in spiritually guiding his or her children?

11. What little things irritate you? What are your expectations regarding them?

12. In regard to our free time, what are your expectations about "together time" and "alone time"?

13. What are your expectations of sleep time? Is it okay to wake you up if I have a problem to discuss? How about sleeping extra on weekends and holidays? What about going to bed at different times?

14. What are your expectations regarding household tasks? Who should do what?

15. Who is in charge? Will we share control or will each of us control certain things like money and disciplining the children? What happens if we can't come to an agreement on an issue?

16. Do you think it's more important to be friends or lovers? What does it mean for marriage partners to be friends? To be lovers? To be both?

Love Potion

#44

Pick a specific time of day. It can be any time. Agree to stop and think of each other at that time for one minute. Think loving, uplifting thoughts and end with a prayer for the other's well-being. (Hint: Figure out some way to remind yourself of the time. If you do forget, do it as soon as you remember.)

Chapter 50

THE BOOMERANG EFFECT

The "Boomerang Effect" happens when one partner shares something personal and the other uses it against him or her later in a fight.

Let's say Lonnie is having some trouble at work. His boss is really on his case. Lonnie comes home to tell his tale of woe to his wife, Cheryl, who is very understanding. Cheryl, in fact, listens and empathizes so well that Lonnie keeps talking until he comes to an insight that his boss has just cause to be on his case because of his lack of organization. Lonnie even admits to goofing off a bit lately.

Fast-forward two weeks. Cheryl and Lonnie are fighting at home over household chores. Cheryl tells Lonnie that the real problem is that he is disorganized and likes to goof off. As proof, she points to the problem at work.

If the fight escalates she might even throw in something like, "Lonnie, you are so lazy and disorganized I wouldn't be surprised if you lost your job. I'm not going to put up with it any more than your boss would!" At this point Lonnie explodes with, "I'm never telling you any of my problems again. You just use them against me!" And he storms out of the room.

Any feelings and thoughts shared in trust in a marriage must be kept sacrosanct. Using them later to condemn the other person undermines trust. And if you take the trust out of the marriage, you remove a major part of the foundation of the marriage.

As tempting as it can be in the heat of battle to use any and all means to win your point, you must not use any information gained in a moment of sharing. If you do, it may help you win the proverbial "battle," but you will also hasten the losing of the "war."

Love Potion

In marriage, if you always wait until you *feel* like doing something, you will end up doing less and less over time. So, practice taking action when your feelings are saying, "Nah, I'd rather not." Here are some things to practice on:

- Making love when you are oh so tired
- Going to church when the covers have a warm grip on you
- Listening when you are preoccupied with your own problems

Chapter 51

Is Your Spouse Still in Love with You?

In the United States, more than one million couples get divorced each year. In some of these divorces, one of the partners gradually became totally disenchanted with the marriage while the other thought all was well.

When you talk to the person who became disenchanted, he typically says, "I tried to tell my spouse for years that I wasn't happy, that things needed to change. But she just wouldn't listen. We would talk a bit, but nothing would ever change. She would just blow me off. Nothing would get resolved. I'm tired of it. This isn't how I want to live the rest of my life. There has to be something better out there and I'm going to go find it."

If you talk to this person's spouse, she says, "I never knew my spouse was so unhappy. I just don't understand it. I thought things were just fine. Sure, we would have our little fights, but we would get over them and things would go on. But we didn't have any major fights. If he was so unhappy, I wish something would have been said sooner. Now I'm being blamed for the marriage falling apart and I don't even know what I did."

Conversations like these take place in marriage counselors' and divorce lawyers' offices thousands of times each year. If the words aren't identical, the thoughts are. One person feels he is in a loveless marriage, while the other is generally satisfied and oblivious to the other's discontent.

The pertinent question for you, then, is "Are you sure your spouse is still in love with you?" This is a question you shouldn't answer yourself. It's a question you need to ask your mate. And I suggest that you don't just ask whether or not he or she loves you. Rather, ask some probing questions that will give you a better idea of your mate's level of marital satisfaction.

If asking questions that may stir up problem areas seems risky to you, then you already have one indication that all isn't well in paradise. It's far better to get things out into the open so you can deal with them than it is to stay in denial and hope the problems will go away. They won't. Time doesn't heal problems. People heal problems. And the only way to heal them is to be aware of them.

At least once a year, couples should check up on each other's level of satisfaction with the other person and with the marriage. It's like going to the dentist for a check-up. It may be a real bother. It may even lead to finding some decay, which in turn leads to a painful root canal. However, this pain is temporary and manageable. If, on the other hand, the check-up isn't done, the decay won't be discovered right away. When the decay grows to a point that it causes pain so intense it can no longer be ignored, it may be too late. The tooth may be lost regardless of your desire to save it.

Like teeth, all marriages have problems once in a while. And, like teeth, these problems will not heal themselves.

Before the problems can be solved, they must first be identified. Here are some questions to help you do a check-up on your marriage. When you ask them, it would be wise to be nondefensive and to use the Rules of Listening.

THE 12 MARITAL CHECK-UP QUESTIONS

1. How do you feel about the amount of time we spend together?
2. Is there anything you would like to change about the things we do together?
3. What do you think about our sex life? Is it satisfying to you? What would you like for us to change?
4. Do you feel like I support you? Is there something I could do to support you better?
5. Do you feel like I do my share of household tasks? Is there something you would like to see me do differently?
6. How do you feel about the amount of love and affection we express to each other? Is there anything you would like us to change in this area?
7. What, if anything, do you think we ought to change about the way we handle our finances?
8. What are your greatest pleasures in life? Are you getting enough pleasure? If not, how can I support your getting more?
9. What is your greatest hope for our future?
10. How do you feel about the number and types of gifts that I give you?
11. When thinking about the way we communicate, are there any changes you would like to see made?
12. Do I say and do things to help you feel: Capable? Appreciated? Respected? Intelligent? Sexy? Attractive?

By the time each of you has asked and listened to the other's responses, you will have a good idea of the state of your marriage. You will also know what changes need to be made. Knowing these things is vital to keeping a marriage together.

Here are two cautions. Once you know the changes your spouse is asking of you and you have agreed to them, then you must make an honest effort to do what you promised. Making commitments to change without following through undermines your marriage. Perfect change isn't required for a marriage to be happy, but an honest effort is!

It's also wise to remember that people's needs and desires change. What once was perfectly acceptable may now be unacceptable. Therefore, do these check-ups at least yearly. When you do so, don't be surprised if some of the answers change.

#46
Love Potion

Use your creativity to write the following Bible verse in such a way that you could frame it and hang it where the two of you can't help but see it every day:

"LOVE IS PATIENT, LOVE IS KIND. IT DOES NOT ENVY, IT DOES NOT BOAST, IT IS NOT PROUD. IT IS NOT RUDE, IT IS NOT SELF-SEEKING, IT IS NOT EASILY ANGERED, IT KEEPS NO RECORD OF WRONGS. LOVE DOES NOT DELIGHT IN EVIL BUT REJOICES WITH THE TRUTH. IT ALWAYS PROTECTS, ALWAYS TRUSTS, ALWAYS HOPES, ALWAYS PERSEVERES. LOVE NEVER FAILS." —1 CORINTHIANS 13:4-7

Chapter 52

IS YOUR MARRIAGE PREPARED TO SURVIVE A CRISIS?

Crises are the furthest things from the minds of newlyweds. All they see are bright, shiny trouble-free futures. This is as it should be. If engaged couples could get any kind of a glimpse at all of the trouble and woe ahead, they might give up on the idea of marriage.

The problem with being blind to the future, though, is that it causes most to be ill prepared to deal with crises. Unfortunately, crises will come sooner or later. Everyone one day has to deal with the deaths of friends and family members. Health problems of all sorts present themselves eventually. Job losses, forced moves, and financial problems can all befall marriages. Just by living life, problems come and go. Some are minor; some are major. But, one thing is clear, if you live long enough you will encounter some problems you cannot fix.

It's our response to these problems that makes a major difference in marriage. Couples happily married for a lifetime learn how to handle crises successfully. They also become familiar with how their mates handle stress and learn how best to support them during the crisis.

Much of this knowledge comes from experience. None of us really knows how we'll handle a major life crisis until the time comes. The good thing is that we can prepare enough so that when a crisis does present itself, it doesn't destroy our marriage.

26 Ways People Respond to Crises

The first thing you can do as a couple to prepare is to talk about how you have seen other people handle crises. In these discussions you can look to acquaintances, friends, and family members. Talk about the severe problems you have seen these people suffer. In particular, identify ways they handled the stress of the situation. Ask yourselves these questions. Did they

1. Seek out a friend or family member to talk to?
2. Refuse to talk?
3. Blame themselves?
4. Blame someone else?
5. Withdraw from friends and family?
6. Drink excessively?
7. Take mood-altering drugs (illicit or prescription)?
8. Escape (in one of the too many ways to list!)?
9. Seek counseling?
10. Get philosophical?
11. Go into denial?
12. Exercise excessively?
13. Diet excessively?
14. Eat excessively?
15. Pray?
16. Get educated about the problem?
17. Seek the best help available?
18. Support friends and family?
19. Have a nervous breakdown?
20. Get depressed?

21. Get angry?
22. Leave?
23. Act like a Pollyanna?
24. Work excessively?
25. Talk excessively (beat the problem to death)?
26. Cry (appropriately or excessively)?

Once you have talked about some ways people you know have handled their crises, discuss how the two of you handle stress. Identify some of the problems you have encountered in the past and what you did to get through them. Then ask each other this question: "How can I best support you when you are going through a very difficult time?"

47
Love Potion

Develop a personal style of saying hello and good-bye to your spouse. Be sure to stop doing whatever you are doing when you say hello and good-bye, and go over to your mate and make loving contact in your special way. Taking the time to do so makes a powerful nonverbal statement that your spouse is extremely important to you.

Chapter 53

THE SECOND-BIGGEST SHOCK

The first big shock in marriage comes when you find out your spouse isn't the absolutely wonderful and perfect person you thought you married. Eventually all couples get hit with the second big shock of their marriage, too: the realization that they consciously will have to do things on a daily basis to help keep the marriage vital.

Unfortunately, many couples never come to this realization. They stay oblivious to this fact even after their divorce. These are the ones who hold on to the myth that if you are in love, everything else will come automatically. Wrong! Even in early romance couples put an enormous amount of effort into making their relationships flourish. It was an everyday task that worked so well it ended in marriage. It may have seemed to come automatically, but in reality both partners put in a great deal of effort to satisfy the other's needs in every way possible.

After the early years of marriage, the everyday tasks of making a living, running a household, and raising a family usurp the place of the romantic activities that keep love alive and satisfying. Even though couples are told this repeatedly, it doesn't sink in or they don't adjust their actions accordingly.

There are several reasons why. Some couples hold tight to the belief that "if we are in love, then everything else will come naturally." These same couples often also believe that if a lot of effort needs to be put into the marriage, this is an indicator that the marriage isn't a very good one and isn't worth saving. Couples that maintain this attitude usually end up in divorce court or a loveless marriage.

Other couples pay lip service—they seemingly agree whole-heartedly, but privately think they are exempt. Having to plan and carry out activities to keep love alive, they think, is for those poor unfortunate people who have lousy marriages. Those who hold this view are in for a huge shock. Hopefully they will realize before it's too late that they too must consciously work on their marriage every single day.

Still others have heard the cliché about marriages being hard work, but they think that's really all it is, just a cliché. What these people often think is that making a living and raising children are much more important. They likely wouldn't admit it to themselves, but doing things to make the marriage work isn't even on their list of priorities. After their divorce, these people often lament, "I just don't understand it. I worked myself to death (at careers or child-rearing). I thought everything was fine. Sure, we had some problems, but I made sure that the important stuff was taken care of. Then, all of a sudden, out of nowhere my spouse said he/she wanted a divorce and that it was my fault. Go figure!"

Happily married and stable couples go through the shock that love isn't automatically forever. Then they get over it. When they recover, they realize they need to add activities of love to their daily list of priorities. At the same time, they understand that it's crucial to put these plans into action regardless of work, household, and child-rearing demands. The couples who do so bypass the heartbreak of divorce and stay happily married for a lifetime.

#48

Love Potion

Surreptitiously, look through some picture albums containing pictures of your spouse when he or she was a child. Pick out your favorite one and have it enlarged and framed. You might even consider having it blown up into a poster (most photo shops can send pictures away and have this done for you). Surprise your spouse with the gift. Tell him or her why you liked that picture so much.

Chapter 54

Do You Say Yes or No Too Much?

Some people say yes too much. Some people say no too much. Too much of saying yes can be harmful if it means you are frequently giving in regardless of your own wishes. Too much of saying no can be harmful if it means you are frequently resisting your spouse's wishes.

Whether either partner is saying yes or no too much is easy to detect. All you have to do is to look at their satisfaction level and whether they're complaining frequently and persistently that their needs aren't being met. If this is the case, there could be a problem. One person may be yielding to or denying the other too often.

The injured spouse may complain to her partner, may talk to a third person, or may engage in negative self-talk. Normally, though, she sublimates her needs in favor of satisfying her husband's needs. This is done in the name of love. After a while, she starts to assert her own desires. If her needs are consistently denied, then she's likely to complain.

If the complaints aren't resolved, they may escalate. They may be expressed in passive-aggressive action, a martyr complex, or persistent nagging and complaining. If she continues to feel her needs aren't being met, sooner or later the marriage will become loveless.

Usually when this happens, the spouse is oblivious. Despite messages from the partner, he thinks everything is fine—after all, his own needs are being met. In marriage counseling he may say, "I knew we had a few problems, but I didn't think they were that bad. My wife complains sometimes, but I thought we had resolved all that. I just don't see what the big problem is."

By the time couples come in for marriage counseling, it's difficult to turn the situation around. The complaining spouse often feels hurt and neglected. She definitely doesn't feel capable, appreciated, respected, intelligent, sexy, and attractive. It's likely, too, that she doesn't hold much hope that meaningful change can or will be made.

Compounding the problem is the likelihood that she no longer feels any love. If this is the case, then her motivation to do the work necessary to turn the marriage around may be low.

Couples who stay happily married find ways to satisfy both their own needs and their partner's. They also realize needs can and do change over time. Therefore, to keep their marriage vital, they identify and satisfy these needs.

In doing so, a fine balance must be struck. On the one hand, mature, mentally healthy people take responsibility for knowing and satisfying their own needs. On the other hand, in a mature and mentally healthy marriage, the partners learn to also identify and satisfy their mate's needs. The common theme is that it's essential for the needs of both partners to be met at some level.

This doesn't mean all needs and desires must be met at all times. This is unreasonable to expect. It also doesn't mean each partner will have similar levels of satisfaction at the same times. It's perfectly normal and common for one spouse to be really satisfied while the other is discontented. This isn't cause to run to the divorce courts.

However, when and if this disparity in satisfaction levels exists in your marriage, you and your spouse must discuss the needs of the partner who is feeling dissatisfied. In fact, many discussions may be required to help you clarify feelings, thoughts, possible plans, and goals. To either not talk about it or to limit the discussion to one or two conversations will likely lead to continual dissatisfaction.

Sincere effort from both partners to help each other have their needs met goes a long way toward keeping a marriage together and happy. This way, if one partner becomes dissatisfied, she feels the support of the spouse. Support and commitment cements marriages for a lifetime.

49
Love Potion

Help your spouse do a needs assessment by going through the following inventory and ranking each item with an "ES" for Extremely Satisfied, an "S" for Satisfied, or an "NI" for Needs Improvement. Go over each item together and ask why he or she answered in that way. Focus on positive areas as well as the negative. In the weeks to come, discuss how unfulfilled needs and desires can be better met. When discussing areas that need improvement, don't assign or assume blame. The rule to remember is to give information without blaming and to listen to information without getting defensive.

THE "HAPPILY MARRIED FOR LIFE NEEDS" ASSESSMENT

_____ 1. Laughter and joy

_____ 2. Romance

_____ 3. Honesty

_____ 4. Gifts

_____ 5. Appreciation

_____ 6. Expressions of caring

_____ 7. Verbal affirmations and compliments

_____ 8. Household chores

_____ 9. Financial management

_____ 10. Generosity

_____ 11. Flexibility

_____ 12. Listening and understanding

_____ 13. Respect

_____ 14. Forgiveness

_____ 15. Security

_____ 16. Intimacy

_____ 17. Playfulness

_____ 18. Trust

_____ 19. Shared vision for the future

_____ 20. Support

The "Happily Married for Life Needs" Assessment is a wonderful tool for couples to use to bolster their marriage. However, it can spark blame and defensiveness. If you experience these reactions, either put the assessment aside for another time or consider seeing a marriage counselor to help you work through the issues that come up.

Chapter 55

WHAT YOU FOCUS ON IS WHAT YOU GET

In the early stages of love, partners do all the right things to make sure that their mates' needs are met. On a daily basis, they go out of their way to make sure their loved one feels capable, appreciated, respected, intelligent, sexy, and attractive.

One powerful way they do this is by focusing on their partner's positive traits and openly admiring them. Things are frequently said like, "You are so considerate. You have such good manners, and the things you do make me feel very special"; or, "You are so outgoing. You are truly a joy to be around. Your energy is infectious!"

These kinds of comments help to fertilize the couple's budding love. They are so powerful in building a strong love foundation that I would like to dissect them so we can look at them in detail.

First of all, it's evident the person giving the compliment takes notice of some behavior. Next, he interprets the behavior to be positive. Then he attributes the behavior to a trait his lover has. This trait is also interpreted as positive. All of this information is formulated into a compliment. In sum, compliments from start to finish look like this:

1. A behavior or set of behaviors is noticed.
2. The behaviors are interpreted as positive.

3. The behaviors are attributed to a positive trait.
4. The above information is formulated into a compliment.
5. The compliment is expressed in a warm and affectionate way.

As powerful as this process is to facilitate the growth and maintenance of love, couples tend to stop using it after awhile. Then the process transforms. It isn't a conscious shift but a major change of focus. For many couples, once their needs aren't being met, they start interpreting behaviors negatively. Then, they attribute the behaviors to negative traits and point out this information. The process is the same, but it's negative in focus. It looks like this:

1. A behavior or set of behaviors is noticed.
2. The behaviors are interpreted as negative.
3. The behaviors are attributed to a negative trait.
4. The above information is formulated into a criticism.
5. The criticism is expressed in a cold and contemptuous way.

The interesting thing is that the very same behavior can go through the compliment process in the early years of love and through the criticism process later. Let's take friendly socializing behavior, for example. When in love, this behavior is likely to go through the compliment process and come out something like, "You sure kept everyone entertained at the party. I admire your ability to mix with people and to make friends." But after a few years of marriage, this same behavior may be met with, "You didn't pay any attention to me last night at the party. All you care about is making friends. You are so self-centered!" The same information is noticed, but the resulting assessment and expression are different.

The reason for the dramatic difference is the focus. When we're in love, our focus is on the positive. For some couples, at least one partner may change to a negative focus. He may feel his needs aren't being met and will then strike out with criticism, thinking this will somehow get her to meet his needs. The thinking here isn't conscious, but it's a very real process nevertheless.

In another marriage, one of the partners may retaliate for perceived criticism. Still others shift from compliments to criticism because that's what they grew up with.

But when it comes down to it, it doesn't matter much why people change their focus. What matters is that they need to become aware of what they are doing and change back to focusing on the positive.

It's critical to the survival and maintenance of a happy marriage that partners interpret each other's actions in a positive way and that they attribute them to positive qualities. To do so is to reinforce both the qualities and the marriage. To do the opposite is to undermine a person's self-esteem and the whole marriage foundation. Research consistently states that people will not stay in a marriage if their partners continually criticize them.

Research by Dr. John Gottman at the University of Washington with two thousand couples also shows that for marriages to be happy, couples need to have at least five positive exchanges for every negative one. The more positive exchanges you have, the happier and more stable your marriage will be.

Love Potion

Look over the following lists of personality traits. Make a commitment to focus on the positive when it comes to behavior that's open to interpretation. Practice on your spouse, your children, and friends. The more you do this for other people, the more they will do it for you. However, to be effective, give your compliments without thought to reciprocation of any kind.

Agreeable	Forthright
Assertive	Friendly
Careful	Giving
Creative	Good-natured
Dependable	Grateful
Direct	Imaginative
Exact	

Chapter 56

KISS AND TELL: PART 4

I t's time to play Kiss and Tell again. If you have been playing this game throughout the book, you most likely are starting to enjoy an increased level of intimacy in your marriage. If so, please write and tell me about it or about any of the other experiences you have had as a result of reading this book and trying the Love Potions. You can e-mail me at larry@smartdiscipline.com. In the meantime, here are some more Kiss and Tell questions.

Here are the instructions. Change them, if you wish, to suit your purposes and relationship, especially if it will make the process of "Kissing and Telling" more fun.

KISS AND TELL INSTRUCTIONS:

1. Flip a coin to see who goes first. The winner decides whether to Kiss or Tell.
2. The Kisser gives the Teller a kiss (preferably passionate) and picks a question to ask.
3. The Kisser listens, following the Rules of Listening (chapter 20).
4. The Teller answers the question to the best of his or her ability.

5. Switch roles. The new Kisser can choose to ask the same question or a different one.

6. Use your sense of humor. Laughter and all forms of encouragement are strongly suggested.

KISS AND TELL QUESTIONS—PART FOUR

1. How important do you think it is in a marriage to be playful? What kinds of playfulness are okay to you and what kinds are not?

2. What one thing do you wish you could unlearn? What do you wish I would unlearn?

3. Why do you think so many couples get divorced?

4. Do you believe in angels?

5. Do you believe in ghosts?

6. Have you ever had a faith experience? If so, tell me about it.

7. What is the most embarrassing thing that happened to you when you were young?

8. What is your proudest memory from your childhood?

9 Who is your favorite cartoon character and why?

10. What do you wish you could understand better?

11. If you had a gift certificate from the mall for one thousand dollars, what would you buy?

12. What did you always look forward to doing with your family?

Love Potion

Give your spouse a gift certificate for a massage. Better yet, take a class in massage together and practice on each other. You might even want to buy a portable massage table and keep it at home. Use soft romantic music, candles, and scents. Take turns on separate evenings. Make it so the one being massaged can totally relax and not have to be responsible for anything else that night.

There are lots of possibilities to give and receive love in this Love Potion. I haven't met anyone yet who wasn't absolutely delighted with a good massage!

Chapter 57

Do You Have the Self-Control and Emotional Maturity to Handle Conflict?

This chapter contains a self-test to see if you have the skills to handle relational conflict in a healthy way. Actually, everyone has this capacity, but many don't know how to access or develop their skills.

The first step in changing anything about you or your love relationship is figuring out what needs to be changed. This test is designed to help you get insight into what you might want to work on to handle conflict better.

The Conflict Readiness Test

Instructions: Answer the following questions true or false. Answer as truthfully as possible. You don't need to show your answers to anyone. You may want to record your answers on a separate sheet of paper to maintain your privacy.

_____ 1. I prefer to avoid conflicts.

_____ 2. When my spouse complains to me, I often complain to him or her about something.

_____ 3. I admit that I can be a bit sarcastic at times.

_____ 4. I don't mean to, but once in a while I make a remark that is insulting to my spouse.

_____ 5. My spouse complains that I make too many excuses.

_____ 6. Everyone knows I have a bad temper.

_____ 7. When my spouse gets on my case, I leave the house.

_____ 8. Once in a while I get my way by putting my spouse on a guilt trip.

_____ 9. Sometimes I find myself thinking about how I can get back at my spouse.

_____ 10. I try to control myself but sometimes I hit something when I get angry.

_____ 11. I'm pretty good at using put-down humor.

_____ 12. For me, keeping the peace is the best way to go about things.

_____ 13. Don't tell anyone, but I use a few recreational drugs to relieve my stress.

_____ 14. I've been known to make a few threats to get people to come around to my way of thinking.

_____ 15. Sometimes I get so frustrated when I am arguing that I bring up all kinds of unrelated issues during the same argument.

_____ 16. Often I find that when other people give me negative feedback, they are way off-base.

_____ 17. If you ever heard me arguing with my spouse, you would hear me shoveling it all back in his or her direction.

_____ 18. I drink to relax. I drink more when my spouse and I are fighting.

_____ 19. I do my fair share of blaming.

_____ 20. If you talked to my spouse, he or she would tell you I whine a lot.

_____ 21. The more my spouse confronts me, the more I clam up.

_____ 22. I hate it, but I tend to pout when I don't get my way.

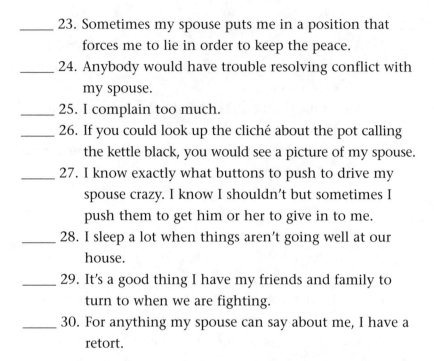

_____ 23. Sometimes my spouse puts me in a position that forces me to lie in order to keep the peace.

_____ 24. Anybody would have trouble resolving conflict with my spouse.

_____ 25. I complain too much.

_____ 26. If you could look up the cliché about the pot calling the kettle black, you would see a picture of my spouse.

_____ 27. I know exactly what buttons to push to drive my spouse crazy. I know I shouldn't but sometimes I push them to get him or her to give in to me.

_____ 28. I sleep a lot when things aren't going well at our house.

_____ 29. It's a good thing I have my friends and family to turn to when we are fighting.

_____ 30. For anything my spouse can say about me, I have a retort.

Now go back and change any answers you weren't totally truthful about. Then stop and think about how you felt when you were answering the questions. Was it a proud feeling? In other words, did you feel you must be pretty good at resolving conflict? Or did you squirm a bit? Did you think the best thing to do was to destroy your answer sheet so no one would see it? If you showed your spouse your answers, which answers would he or she disagree with?

Scoring instructions: This self-test is also self-assessed. You either pass or fail according to the grade you give yourself. Please realize, though, that this instrument is meant to give you some insights into ways that you might change how you deal with conflict.

Love Potion

Have your spouse take this test and answer the questions about you from his or her perspective. Rarely do we get an honest look at ourselves, so this is a good opportunity to get some feedback. Ask him or her to be as honest as possible and to give you the scoring sheet when finished. Ask your spouse to explain his or her answers. Listen without making defensive remarks and say thank you at the end.

COMMUNICATION MISTAKES THAT CAN RUIN YOUR MARRIAGE

I asked my wife, Nydia, one day at lunch what she felt was the most important ingredient of a happy marriage. She said, "Well, if I had to pick one thing, I would say it's communication." When I asked why, she replied, "Because everything depends on communication. I mean communication is a daily affair. You can't do it one day and not the next. You constantly have to talk with your spouse. If you do it badly, nothing else will go right either."

Smart person, my wife. She put the critical nature of communication succinctly. The quality of communication in a marriage determines the quality of the relationship. They are in direct relation to each other.

This isn't good news for many couples. For some, the wish is that somehow the marriage will work if they make enough money or focus on the kids or become successful in their careers or if they have a great sex life. Sorry. None of these will matter much if the partners don't lick their communication problems.

But how do you know if you have a communication problem? Most often it's easy—just listen to your spouse. If you have a problem, he or she has most likely been telling you about it for quite a while. But because of the communication problem, you probably haven't "heard" or at least believed what your spouse has been saying. So you may not know that you have a problem, or if you do, the severity of it.

Here's a test you and your spouse can take to help determine if you have a problem. It will also give you an indication of the severity of the communication problem.

THE COMMUNICATION TEST

Instructions: Give the following questions a score between zero and ten. If you feel your spouse never does this, score it a zero. If he or she does it a lot, score it a ten. Or score it somewhere between the two depending on how you would rank the frequency or severity of the behavior. Make sure to score the test based on your spouse's communication behavior, not your own.

_____ 1. My spouse doesn't stop and look at me when I am talking.

_____ 2. Sometimes my spouse ridicules what I say.

_____ 3. My mate often tries to talk me into changing my feelings.

_____ 4. Sometimes my spouse calls me names.

_____ 5. When I try to talk about problems, my spouse tries to change the subject.

_____ 6. My spouse always has an excuse.

_____ 7. My spouse often pouts if I bring up problems.

_____ 8. When my spouse and I argue, I often end up feeling demeaned.

_____ 9. My spouse is prone to exaggerating.

_____ 10. My spouse lies or tells half-truths.

_____ 11. My spouse is dogmatic.

_____ 12. My spouse insists on looking at things logically.

_____ 13. My spouse won't listen to me if I look at things logically.

_____ 14. My spouse loses his or her temper when we argue.

_____ 15. My partner blows me off.

_____ 16. If I don't give in to my spouse, he or she won't give me any peace until I do.

_____ 17. My partner likes to play psychologist with me (analyzes my motives).

_____ 18. My spouse brings up past mistakes when we argue.

_____ 19. My spouse refuses to take any responsibility.

_____ 20. My spouse knows my "hot buttons" and doesn't hesitate to push them.

To score this test, see if you rated any of the items over a five. If so, your communication with your spouse is less than ideal and needs work. This isn't uncommon, so don't feel bad about it. What is common in marriages is to have several areas that need work. Most of this work can be accomplished relatively easily if both partners are open to giving and receiving honest feedback and to committing to change. The exercises in the "The Art of Settling Arguments" chapters will help.

However, if you scored several items eight or above, your communication problem may be severe enough to warrant outside help. There's no shame in seeking counseling. Communication problems can destroy relationships. Bad communication results in anger, hurt, and resentment that can build to intolerable levels. Without help, these feelings can be insurmountable. If you feel this is the case with you, before you call a divorce lawyer, call a marriage counselor.

To find a good marriage counselor, ask your friends, pastor or rabbi, or doctor which marriage counselors in your area get good results. Try, if you can, to find someone who is licensed and who specializes in marriage counseling. If the first counselor you find can't help you, try someone else. When people have a physical problem, they go to a doctor. If that doctor doesn't get results, they find another that can.

Love Potion

Change one bad habit you know annoys your spouse. Just one. Commit to trying the change for one month. If the habit annoys your spouse, it's likely a nuisance to you at some level as well. So, for one month stop smoking, eat less, stop drinking, use better manners, work less, dress or eat better. Whatever it is, just do it!

HOW TO CHANGE LOUSY COMMUNICATION PATTERNS: PART 1

NEGATIVE FEELINGS, COMPLAINING, LEAVING IN ANGER, AND DEFENSIVENESS

Good communication is central to being happily married for a lifetime. It's through good communication patterns that our spouse may come to feel capable, appreciated, respected, intelligent, sexy, and attractive. If it's lacking, he may come to feel incompetent, disrespected, dull, unappealing, and unattractive. One way of connecting with your spouse will lead to a great marriage, the other to a loveless marriage or the divorce courts.

The path then to a great marriage would seem simple: Do a good job of communicating and marital bliss is assured. The trouble comes in carrying it out! While the intention to do so can be sincere, putting good communication into practice can be tricky.

The following communication patterns can lead to severe marital problems if they aren't corrected. Following each problem is a strategy, or solution, for correcting poor communication. Please keep in mind you are only in control of your own communication patterns. Don't make the mistake of pointing out your spouse's communication errors. While it's okay to give information about how his attitude makes you feel, it isn't okay to instruct him in the ways of proper communication. To do so will come across badly and will be counterproductive. The best way to help your spouse communicate more productively is to do so yourself.

COMMUNICATION PROBLEM: FEELING EXTREMELY NEGATIVE
SOLUTION: POSTPONE TALKING ABOUT THE ISSUE WITH YOUR SPOUSE

Sometimes we lock onto a negative feeling. When we do, everything we say is likely to flow out of that feeling. One example is jealousy, which very often is felt intensely. For as long as we feel an intense emotion like this, much of what we say will be colored—even directed—by that emotion. This isn't good. Brain research indicates that when people are feeling intense emotions, access to the logical side of their brains is cut off. This means we are acting purely on emotion.

When you're stuck in negative feelings like this, you're likely to say things that will damage the relationship. You're also likely to say and do things that will only escalate the fight.

The solution is to recognize when you're stuck in a negative feeling and to refuse to allow yourself the luxury of talking with your spouse then. Talk with a friend, counselor, or family member about your feelings. Talk with anyone who is willing to let you rant and rave and get it all out. Once you have done so, give it a little time to make sure you are no longer in the grip of the emotion before you talk with your spouse.

Also, when a negative emotion grabs hold of your mind and refuses to leave, it can be very helpful to enter into prayer or meditation. This can be difficult too, because sometimes emotions drown out any positive thoughts. If this happens, here is one of the most powerful ways I know to regain control of your emotions and enter into contact with God.

Take some time to sit down away from other people and distractions like the telephone or television. Sit in a straight back chair with your feet on the floor and your hands resting in your lap. Close your eyes and breathe in and out normally. As you breathe in, silently say to yourself, "Come, Holy Spirit." When you breathe out, silently say, "Quicken within us." When you breathe back in, say to yourself, "Fill our hearts with love." On your next breath out, start over with, "Come, Holy Spirit," then, "Quicken within us," as you breathe in, followed with, "Fill our hearts with love," as you breathe out. Continue to do this for five to ten minutes. If negative thoughts intrude, don't worry about it. Continue the process anyway. Please note: Say "us" and "our" instead of "me" and "my" as this extends your prayer to all those who are involved in the situation.

After five to ten minutes (perhaps sooner) you will find your emotions starting to heal. When you feel calmer, open your eyes. You will find that while negative thoughts may still intrude, you will feel more in control and able to find positive solutions to the situation at hand. I have had people report seemingly miraculous healings to impossible situations after doing this as well.

In especially rough times, you may want to repeat this healing meditation four times throughout your day for just a few minutes each time. You can even do it at your desk, while waiting in line, or anywhere you have a spare moment. The more you put this meditative prayer into action, the more you will find that all kinds of things will start going your way. Life will become easier and emotions will become more manageable. As you increasingly invite the Holy Spirit into your life and marriage, you may also notice all kinds of wonderful, even miraculous things, taking place in your life and in the lives of those around you. *(Please note: As you use this healing meditation/prayer, we would appreciate it if you would share your experiences and healings with us so we can share them with others. Please e-mail me at larry@smartdiscipline.com.)*

COMMUNICATION PROBLEM: MOANING AND GROANING, NAGGING
SOLUTION: REPLACE THE HABIT OF COMPLAINING WITH A HABIT OF FOCUSING ON THE POSITIVE

If you are someone who complains about anything and everything, stop it! It will ruin your marriage and your life. For as long as you are complaining, your life will be unmanageable and unhappy. Most complainers picked up this bad habit in childhood and have continued into their adult life. This is too bad, because people don't like to be around someone who is always complaining.

Unfortunately, this isn't an easy habit to break—the Israelites were condemned to wandering in the desert for forty years for their grumbling, complaining ways. Chronic complaining becomes deeply ingrained and the chief way the person deals with her world.

To change this habit—and yes, complaining *is* a habit—will take some concerted effort. The only way I know of to change a negative habit is to replace it with a positive one. If you just stop doing something without having a replacement for it, you will most likely fill the void with something else. To make sure this something else is of benefit you, make a decision to establish a habit of pointing out the positive and expressing gratitude for it both to people and to God. You may know people who sincerely say, "Thank you, Jesus," when something good happens. These are people who have a habit of focusing on and expressing gratitude for the good in their lives.

Here is the rule to keep in mind: Whatever you focus on increases. If you focus on the positive, you will find good things happening more frequently in your life. If you constantly focus on the negative, you will likely find yourself experiencing more and more negativity. The good thing is that after you make the change to focusing on the positive, you will find the positive will increase in your marriage as well as in your life in general.

COMMUNICATION PROBLEM: GETTING ANGRY OR FRUSTRATED AND LEAVING
SOLUTION: TAKE A BREAK

Some people walk out when they get angry or frustrated in a marital argument. They deal with their negative emotions by physically or emotionally withdrawing.

If this describes you, instead of walking or zoning out, inform your spouse you need to take a short break. When you are calm and feeling good, explain that when you are angry or frustrated, you get an overwhelming urge to leave. Tell him you realize this doesn't solve anything and often makes matters worse. Say that from now on, when you start to feel over-whelmed, you aren't going to leave. Instead, you will explain that you need a thirty-minute break from the discussion, after which time you will be willing to come back and discuss the issue further.

I'm not saying this is easy. However, walking out on arguments—whether by physically walking out of the room or by withdrawing emotionally and refusing to deal with the problem—will one day lead to either divorce or a loveless mar-riage. So it's worth the effort to commit to resolving problems. But give yourself a break. When you start to feel overwhelmed, let your spouse know you need some time alone and you will then come back later to talk the situation through (be sure to give a time frame, such as the thirty minutes suggested above).

COMMUNICATION PROBLEM: HYPERSENSITIVITY AND DEFENSIVENESS
SOLUTION: PRACTICE ASKING QUESTIONS AND CLARIFYING THOUGHTS AND FEELINGS

Are you one of the many people who can't stand to be criticized? If you are, then the level of your happiness will be greatly enhanced if you change. As long as you allow yourself to get hurt and defensive whenever your spouse expresses a negative thought, your marriage and your own happiness will suffer.

In every marriage, change needs to be negotiated. For it to take place, both partners must be open to discussing problems. This process is thwarted if one of the partners is hypersensitive and defensive.

To become less hypersensitive takes more than telling yourself that from now on you aren't going to be defensive. Rather, you will need a plan of action. The best one I know of is to practice asking questions and clarifying thoughts and feelings.

It's good to start this practice when your spouse is talking to you about neutral issues that don't give rise to any negative feelings. Practice on something like the news or what is happening at his or her work. Ask questions and clarify what your spouse is thinking and feeling. When you get good at it, start doing the same when you begin to feel hurt and/or defensive in a conversation. Practice this on both your spouse and on other people in your life.

Put off expressing your own views and feelings. Instead, focus solely on your partner's views and feelings. With practice, you'll notice that you are no longer so hypersensitive or defensive when your spouse complains to you about something.

This is worthwhile to do for yourself and your marriage. It will greatly increase your enjoyment in life and your self-esteem. But it takes lots of practice. And while practicing, you need to have patience with yourself and realize that you will make mistakes.

COMMUNICATION PATTERNS: PART 2

BLAMING, FAULT–FINDING, CONTEMPT, AND SARCASM

The following two communication problems have in common negative, critical thinking. However, the second problem is far more serious.

COMMUNICATION PROBLEM: BLAMING AND FAULT-FINDING
SOLUTION: GIVE NONCRITICAL INFORMATION AND MAKE A REQUEST

When one partner habitually blames his spouse for problems, the level of marriage satisfaction is low. As human beings, our egos, self-esteem, and self-confidence are eroded if someone frequently blames us and points out our faults. If this condition exists in a marriage, one of two courses is typically pursued. The person being blamed will either exit the marriage or will stay in it, refuse to cooperate, and try to make the other person as miserable as she feels.

The solution is to reduce your complaints to basic information. Here are some examples:

Instead of: "You never listen to me."

Say: "Right now I don't think you are listening to me. Would you take a moment to sit down and talk with me?"

Instead of: "You are so messy. You have no consideration."
Say: "Your socks are on the floor. I feel angry when you leave
them there. Would you please pick them up?"

Instead of: "We are late again and it's your fault."
Say: "We are late. I really dislike being late. Would you
please do a better job of being on time?"

Doing this will help you eliminate criticism and blame,
which only serve to undermine relationships. By just giving
information followed by a polite request, you are much more
likely to get what you want and to preserve your love.

COMMUNICATION PROBLEM: CONTEMPT AND SARCASM
SOLUTION: GET SOME HELP

Here's the grim truth. If one of the partners in the marriage
shows contempt for the other, the relationship is in deep trouble. Current research says the marriage will end within three
years. This is a 97 percent certainty, according to research done
at the University of Washington. Even if it does survive, if dramatic changes aren't taken, the marriage will be unsatisfactory
for both parties. Truth be known, it will likely be a living hell.

Such a marriage will take some major help from a marriage
counselor to turn it around. It is extremely rare for couples to
turn the situation around by themselves. Even with help it will
take a major commitment from both partners. But getting help
and making this commitment is a heck of a lot cheaper financially and emotionally than getting a divorce.

There's one other reason to do what it takes to face and overcome this problem in your marriage: Problems follow people. If

you are having this problem in your current marriage, odds are if you don't successfully address it you will end up with the same problem in another relationship. If you are the person showing the contempt, you will probably do the same in your next marriage. If you are on the receiving end, you will likely marry someone who will treat you with similar contempt. While there are always exceptions, this happens to the majority, even when people swear they won't remarry into the same situation.

One thing is virtually guaranteed. When contempt exists between partners, the marriage will end either legally or emotionally. Just as certainly, in order to save the marriage, outside help must be sought. If your partner won't agree to go with you, then go yourself. But go. Doing so may save your marriage.

Chapter 61

COMMUNICATION PATTERNS: PART 3

PLACATING AND SUBVERTING YOUR OWN NEEDS

You might think that the spouse who goes to any lengths to always make peace and give in to the other partner would be a saint and the marriage a healthy one. Nothing could be further from the truth.

COMMUNICATION PROBLEM: PLACATING, SUBVERTING YOUR NEEDS
SOLUTION: IDENTIFY NEEDS AND NEGOTIATE

In marriages, it's destructive if one person continually gives in to the other in order to keep peace. It's very destructive, in fact. This surprises those who do it, because they placate their mates in order to keep the marriage together. Their fear is that if they don't give in to their mate's wishes, there will be trouble. This fear is so real and so great that they think not giving in will lead perhaps to the marriage's demise.

In reality, placating just reinforces a dysfunctional marital communication pattern, one in which one marriage partner demands, often angrily, that things be done her way, and, in response, her partner gives in and sublimates his own needs. Often, he rationalizes his submission to be for "the good of the family."

Whenever this pattern is acted out, it's reinforced. The demanding person develops a habit of asserting her will through anger or threats. The submissive person gets into a habit of maintaining peace by giving in. A common scenario goes like this:

> **Wife:** I'm going shopping with my friend Sue on Saturday.
> **Husband:** I thought we agreed we were taking the kids to the zoo on Saturday.
> **Wife:** I changed my mind. You take the kids to the zoo. I'm going shopping!
> **Husband:** I don't think that's fair. I really want us to go as a family.
> **Wife:** Tough. If you don't like it, I might just go shopping on Sunday, too. In fact, I think I will do just that.
> **Husband:** Fine. Whatever you want to do is okay with me.

Or another scenario (to show I'm not gender-biased) might go like this:

> **Husband:** I won't be home for supper tonight.
> **Wife:** Again?
> **Husband:** Yes, again. I have to work for a living, remember?
> **Wife:** I thought we might spend an evening together for a change.
> **Husband:** Yeah, right. Why don't you call your mother? The two of you are joined at the hip anyway.
> **Wife:** Okay, okay. I'll wait up for you.
> **Husband:** Don't bother.

In both of these scenarios anger is apparent. So are the threats that the situation will escalate into a painful verbal battle if the conversations continue. To prevent this from happening, the placater gives in. Anything, they think, is better that having to deal with an angry outburst.

This process is destructive because one person gets used to having his needs met at the expense of his spouse. Love, in such a situation, dies. The aggressive person loses all respect for the submissive one. As for the submissive partner, several things happen: self-respect is lost, needs go unmet, anger builds, and passive-aggressive actions are taken.

While it's a loving thing to sometimes sublimate your own needs in favor of your mate's, it's only functional if it's being done as an act of love. If it's being done continually as a means of keeping peace, then it's destructive to the marriage.

If you use anger to get your way, start practicing sublimating your needs to your spouse's as an act of love. Also, make a commitment to find ways other than anger to express your needs and desires. While doing this, don't allow yourself to use anger or threats in any form to get your way.

If you are the placater, practice identifying, expressing, and negotiating to get your needs met. This can be tough, as many placaters have low self-esteem and self-confidence. If this is true about you, get some counseling or self-help tapes and books. Follow the suggestions until you get to the point where you can negotiate having your needs met despite the potential for anger and arguments. What can help immediately is to use statements and questions such as "I understand that you really want to go shopping. I want us to go to the zoo as a family. Do you think we can find some middle ground?" Or, "I understand that you need to work late tonight. However, I really want us to spend some quality time together soon. What do you think we can do to make that happen?"

Chapter 62

COMMUNICATION PATTERNS: PART 4

THIRD–PARTY COMPLAINING, THROWING IN THE KITCHEN SINK

In this chapter, we look at the destructive patterns of complaining to friends and family about spouses and throwing in the kitchen sink.

COMMUNICATION PROBLEM: THIRD-PARTY COMPLAINING
SOLUTION: COMPLAIN ONLY TO YOUR SPOUSE

It's good to have someone other than your spouse to talk with over your problems. Sometimes a friend or family member can provide both understanding and empathy that can greatly ease your mind and support you. Seeking out and developing a support system outside of your marriage is definitely a wise thing to do. As Scott Peck says, "Life is tough." The more people you have in your support system, the easier it will be to face life's challenges.

That being said, there's also a downside to having a good support system outside of your marriage. The problem comes when one or both people in the marriage get into the habit of talking their problems over with other people rather than with their spouses. This is understandable, especially if one of these friends or family members is really good at listening and empathizing. It's even more understandable if the spouse is lousy at communication.

When people feel they need to go outside their marriages to find solace, trouble lies ahead. One clear danger is that they will fall in love with the person who gives it to them. Another danger is that they conclude that intimacy cannot be had in their marriages and so the marriage is worthless to them.

If you have come to rely on talking problems over with someone other than your spouse, make a commitment to change. Some people find prayer or journaling helpful alternatives, and such options can offer the much-needed outlet that other people have filled. Above all, decide to find ways to improve communication with your spouse until your needs for understanding and intimacy are met within the marriage. While you are doing this, cut your complaining to family and friends to a bare minimum.

COMMUNICATION PROBLEM: THROWING IN THE KITCHEN SINK
SOLUTION: CONSCIOUS COMMITMENT TO DO AWAY WITH BLAME, FAULT-FINDING, AND BRINGING UP MISTAKES FROM THE PAST

One common bad practice in marital communication is when a couple starts to argue and one of the partners brings up every mistake the other has ever made in the marriage. Here is a sample of what I mean:

> **Husband:** Can you please hurry a little bit? The movie starts in thirty minutes and you know how much I hate to miss the beginning.
>
> **Wife:** Well, you were the one that made us late last week for my office party, so get off my back.
>
> **Husband:** You know perfectly well that was your fault, too. I would have been on time but you made me stop off to pick up your dry cleaning. But that's the

way it is with you. You have no insight into your
own faults. Like the time you made us late for my
sister's wedding. We missed the whole ceremony.
How embarrassing!

Wife: What does that have to do with going to the
movie? That's ancient history.

Husband: It has everything to do with it. You just don't
have any consideration for anyone else. You are so
self-centered. Like last Christmas. That's a perfect
example. I wanted to go over to my brother's, but
no, you sat around and pouted until I gave in and
went ice skating with you. Thanks to you I caught a
cold, but did you care? Not in the least. But why
should you? You don't care about anyone but yourself anyway.

The conversation could go on and on. At least, that is, until
the couple gets divorced.

The common recognizable symptoms of the throwing-in-
the-kitchen-sink communication pattern are blame,
fault-finding, and bringing up sins from the past. People use
this pattern for three reasons. First, they use it to get their
way. Because of the barrage of negative information, their
spouses are likely to capitulate in order to end the barrage.
Second, people use it to vent unresolved anger and hurt from
the past. Third, it's used simply because it's a pattern learned
from their parents.

Whatever the reason, it must be stopped if the couple has
any hope of being happily married for a lifetime. To quit, the
person doing it must commit to discussing only the issue at
hand. He must leave off all blame, fault-finding, and bringing

up past mistakes. How does he make these changes? By consciously deciding to be aware of what he is saying and mustering every bit of willpower possible to maintain self-control. This isn't easy, I realize, but to continue to "throw in the kitchen sink" is to condemn the marriage.

COMMUNICATION PATTERNS: PART 5

YES/BUT–ING AND GUILT TRIPS

COMMUNICATION PROBLEM: YES/BUT-ING
SOLUTION: LISTEN, CLARIFY, AND BE ACCOUNTABLE

Yes/but-ing another person is designed to ward off criticism and responsibility. It's a common pattern in marital communication and it goes something like this:

> **Wife:** Could you please make sure you get home on time tonight? We have to leave for the party by seven.
>
> **Husband:** Sure, but why are you on my case? You made us late last time.
>
> **Wife:** Yes, but there was a good reason for that.
>
> **Husband:** Sure, but you always have a good reason. When it comes to my reasons, they are never good enough.
>
> **Wife:** Yes, but …
>
> **Husband:** Sure, but …

In this conversation, both husband and wife are playing the yes-but game. It leads to nowhere and is clearly a no-win situation. The common elements of the yes-but game are refusal to take responsibility and pointing to past mistakes made by the other person.

To intervene and end this bad communication pattern, it requires the commitment of one of the partners to take responsibility. Instead of saying yes-but, the person says, "Yes, I will be sure to be home on time. I know how important it is to you that we leave for the party by seven." The elements of this healthy communication pattern are commitment and clarification. In other words, the person clarifies the other's request, agrees to it, and acknowledges the importance.

Here are some examples:

Husband: I don't like it when I'm the one that has to put the kids to bed every night. How about you doing it sometimes?

Wife: I appreciate it when you put the kids to bed. It frees me up to clean up the kitchen. However, I hear what you are saying about feeling a bit frustrated with taking the bedtime responsibilities night after night.

Husband: Yeah. Actually, I really like doing it. But sometimes I do get tired of it. Especially on nights like tonight when the kids were so hyper.

Wife: What can I do to help?

Husband: Listening to me helps a lot. I guess once in a while I would like to trade responsibilities. You know, I do the kitchen and you put the kids to bed.

Wife: I don't see why not. How about trading tomorrow night? We could even trade every other night if you want.

To communicate in a more functional pattern takes both partners laying aside blame and defensiveness. These must be consciously replaced with a willingness to make requests, clarify needs, and negotiate a solution that is acceptable to both. It can be done. The keys are willingness and consciousness.

COMMUNICATION PROBLEM: GUILT TRIPS, POUTING, AND SULKING
SOLUTION: MAKE A REQUEST AND NEGOTIATE WITHOUT THE USE OF
GUILT, POUTING, OR SULKING

Mothers are famous for putting guilt trips on their children in order to gain compliance. For a husband or wife to use the same method to gain compliance from a spouse is dysfunctional. A typical example of this communication pattern makes it easy to see why.

> **Wife:** What would you like to do this weekend?
> **Husband:** I thought I would go fishing with Joe and Steve.
> **Wife:** You left me alone last weekend. I get so lonely when you are gone, I can't stand it.
> **Husband:** But I went over to my brother's last weekend because you went shopping with your mother. You were only alone for a couple of hours.
> **Wife:** You just don't understand. This house is so big and empty when you are gone. Not only do I get lonely but I get frightened too. If you loved me, you would stay home this weekend and do something with me instead.

Most guilt trips can be identified by one person using the words "if you loved me" somewhere in the conversation. Also, one person is blamed for how the other feels. Decisions are then based on guilt. If the person doesn't get her way, she will probably pout and sulk in order to further her cause.

What a mess! There's no place for guilt trips in a happy, mature marriage. The only solution is to stop them. If you are the person using them, stop it! State your needs and make requests. But leave off the guilt trip.

For example:

Wife: What would you like to do this weekend?

Husband: I thought I would go fishing with Joe and Steve.

Wife: I really wanted to spend the weekend with you. Is there some way we can work that out?

Husband: What did you have in mind?

Wife: I don't know. I would just like you and me to find something to do together. I really don't care so much what we do as long as we are together.

Husband: I like to be with you too. How about I go fishing on Saturday morning and spend the rest of the weekend with you?

Wife: Sounds good to me. Let's make some plans to do something fun.

Is this kind of communication realistic? Sure it is. In fact, it occurs daily in happy marriages. To make them an everyday part of your marriage takes a conscious effort to state your needs and negotiate an outcome without the use of guilt, sulking, or pouting.

Love Potion

Take a risk. Talk to your spouse about something you have had on your mind but have been reluctant to bring up. Broach the subject with a positive attitude and maintain it even if your spouse responds negatively. If the response is negative, resist the urge to cut off the conversation or strike back. Instead, listen and see if you can clarify your spouse's position. If you can do this, you will likely find that your spouse becomes much more understanding of your position as well.

Chapter 64

DO YOU NEED A MARRIAGE COUNSELOR?

Before continuing, take this self-quiz. (Hint: Don't read ahead. Reading the comments will skew the results.)

Put an "X" by the traits you feel describe your spouse. Be honest. Mark both the positive and the negative traits. For privacy, use a separate sheet to record your answers.

PARTNER DESCRIPTION INVENTORY

Accountable	Caring	Dishonest
Agreeable	Childish	Dogmatic
Altruistic	Cold	Dull
Amiable	Complimentary	Encouraging
Annoying	Connected	Exact
Appreciative	Conscious	Fair
Arrogant	Controlled	Forgiving
Assured	Controlling	Forthright
Available	Creative	Fragile
Blatant	Critical	Friendly
Boorish	Dangerous	Gentle
Brash	Dependable	Giving
Bright	Depressed	Good-natured
Careful	Discouraging	Grateful

Hateful	Open	Spiritual
Imaginative	Open-minded	Spontaneous
Impatient	Overbearing	Stable
Inappropriate	Patient	Stingy
Inflexible	Persuasive	Supportive
Insensitive	Philosophical	Tense
Intelligent	Playful	Thoughtful
Interested	Precise	Thrifty
Intrusive	Righteous	Trusting
Inviting	Sanctimonious	Unconscious
Jealous	Self-assured	Uncontrolled
Kind	Self-confident	Unforgiving
Logical	Selfish	Unreliable
Loving	Sensitive	Unyielding
Mild-mannered	Shy	Warm
Modest	Sincere	Weak
Objective	Soothing	Wise

Now that you've marked your spouse's characteristics, go back and put a "P" by the positive ones and an "N" by the negative ones. Use your own judgment to determine which are positive and which are negative. If the trait is admirable to you, mark it positive, if it's something you wish your spouse would change, then mark it negative.

Next, total how many positive and how many negative traits there are. The total number doesn't matter. What matters is the prevailing way you view your spouse. In happy marriages, couples view each other as having mostly positive traits. This doesn't mean they don't recognize their partner's faults. On the contrary, they are aware of them but see them as being outweighed by good traits. (Ask a couple headed to divorce court to take this same test and their lists will be loaded with negative traits.)

As marriages progress, each person chooses to view the other in a primarily positive or negative light. Once the focus is chosen, evidence is sought to support a bias for or against a spouse. For example, if you see your partner positively, then you will find evidence to support the conclusion that he or she has positive traits. You praise that positive evidence to your spouse. At the same time, you ignore or downplay evidence to the contrary.

It goes something like this. A husband notices his wife is neat and organized. He decides this is a positive trait. Then he points out the evidence to his spouse of how neat and organized she is and expresses appreciation for it. When he notices a time when she is sloppy or disorganized, he either ignores it or rationalizes it away as an aberration.

The opposite happens if a decision has been reached that the spouse has negative traits. In the same scenario, the husband notices his wife is neat and organized. He decides this is a negative trait. He interprets time spent cleaning as obsessive and complains to his wife that she is a "neat freak." When she is sloppy, he ignores it or rationalizes it away as an aberration.

What's important here is the positive or negative focus or slant that's chosen. It will determine the level of happiness in the marriage, which in turn will probably determine whether the couple stays together. Couples that choose a positive focus reinforce each other's positive traits. Couples with a negative focus reinforce each other's negative traits. So, behavior in the marriage gets either better or worse, depending on the couple's focus.

If one or both of you focus on the negative, it will be tough for you to turn this around without help. If the marriage is to survive and be happy, then you need to seek out a qualified marriage counselor. Getting help requires putting your ego aside and investing both time and money. But divorce is a much bigger blow to your ego, time, and pocketbook than marriage counseling will ever be.

#55
Love Potion

Send your spouse a gift at work. It doesn't matter what it is, but make it showy. The idea is to create a big stir among his or her workmates. Envy is the name of the game. Go for a lot of "oohs and ahs." This will do wonders for helping your spouse feel cared about and appreciated. Enjoy the rewards at home that night!

Chapter 65

WHY PEOPLE RESIST MARRIAGE COUNSELING

Sometimes, if a marriage is to be saved, counseling is necessary. It's especially necessary if either partner has emotionally withdrawn from the marriage, if there has been an affair, or if one of the partners is focused on the negative traits of his spouse. All three circumstances are very difficult for people to address on their own. It may not be impossible for them to do so, but the likelihood of success is low.

When it comes to marriage counseling, often one or both of the partners are resistant to the idea. The resistance is usually founded on one of several attitudes people typically have about marriage counseling.

One common attitude is that counseling is expensive and probably not worth the cost. It's true that counseling is expensive. Even if you have insurance to cover it, there's still a chance you'll have to pay up to 50 percent of the cost out of your own pocket. As each session can run anywhere from $60 to $150, this can run into a lot of money. People in counseling average eight sessions, so the out-of-pocket cost if you have insurance could run between $240 and $600. If you don't have insurance it would be double these figures. However, the cost could exceed these figures if you needed to go more than eight times.

But whatever the costs, they are far less than the costs of getting a divorce. Legal costs can and do run into the thousands of dollars. The financial burden of establishing two households is also high. And then, there are the costs of selling off joint assets. Finally, one of the partners will probably have to pay child support or alimony. Even if you are on the receiving end of the alimony and child support, it will usually be far less than what is needed to run the household the way it was run during the marriage. Compared to all of these costs, marriage counseling is a bargain.

Another reason people resist marriage counseling is because they feel their spouse is only using the counseling as a means of ambushing them. They fear that the counselor and their spouse will gang up on them to make them out to be the bad person. While one or both people in counseling may try to paint their partners in a negative light, a good counselor will intervene. Nothing is gained in counseling by assigning blame, and most counselors are skilled at moving people away from blame and into more productive ways of dealing with the couple's marital problems.

Then too, there's the fear people have that they are being drawn into marriage counseling only because their spouse wants to end the marriage and feels the counselor can both justify and facilitate this process. If this fear is present, then it should be voiced so the counselor can deal with it directly. It may be that ending the marriage is one of the partner's reasons for entering into counseling. Whether it is or not, it's good to get the issue out into the open so it can be dealt with.

A closely related issue that causes people to refuse to enter into counseling has its foundation in the feeling that "if you need counseling, then there's no use in continuing the marriage." This is particularly true for perfectionists, who need to keep everything in their world orderly, neat, and controlled. Marriage isn't this way and never will be. While this attitude keeps many people from trying counseling, it shouldn't. If anything, counseling should help them satisfy their needs for order, neatness, and control.

Some people, when asked by their spouses to enter into marriage counseling, put a condition on their participation. They try to bargain by saying they will only go to counseling if their mates will guarantee they will stay in the marriage and not seek a divorce. Some spouses are more than willing to make this commitment. If so, that's fine. If they aren't, however, this deal can end the marriage counseling before it starts. The trouble is that the person demanding the guarantee has set up a self-fulfilling prophecy. By demanding something that his spouse is unwilling to agree to, he is facilitating the end of the marriage. Anyone with this attitude should back away from it and give counseling a try with no strings attached. Doing so will at least be giving the marriage a chance at survival.

There are myriad other reasons people resist counseling. They include not wanting to admit failure, not wanting to air "dirty laundry" in front of a stranger, and not believing there's a problem severe enough to warrant counseling. All of these reasons cause people to say no to counseling. Instead, they plead with their spouses to "work it out together." Sometimes this is effective. If the one suggesting the counseling agrees to working the problem out in private, he can also suggest counseling, should the problems not be worked out by some set future time.

Last, I think the biggest reason people resist marriage counseling is because they are afraid. They are afraid of the emotional pain they might have to go through. They are afraid of the painful things they might have to talk about. And they are afraid to face the changes that marriage counseling might lead to. When committing to marriage counseling, there are many unknowns. It's uncharted territory, and people enter into it full of fears. It isn't easy to do. However, many who take the chance are able to improve their marriages dramatically.

#56
Love Potion

Get out of your ruts. Commit to doing one thing differently each day next week. One night sleep on each other's side of the bed, one morning make love, one evening play a game, one week-day evening go out to a movie, one weekend go hiking, one day act on an impulse, and one day go dancing. Or do anything you like. But make them different from your usual activities and habits.

Take turns deciding what those things are. Make a commitment to going along with them even if you don't feel like it. Also, give each other permission to do something different with-out an expectation that it's going to work out perfectly.

Chapter 66

WHAT TO DO IF YOUR SPOUSE IS ADDICTED TO ALCOHOL OR DRUGS

Alcoholism and drug addiction destroy families. I know of no other conditions that take more of a toll on marriages. Throughout my years in the counseling profession I have seen many couples go through years of pain and agony brought on by the behavior that accompanies addictions. Many of these marriages—in fact, most—end in divorce. Yet even then the pain and agony don't end. The addicts, once divorced, drink more or take more drugs and their behavior worsens. Much of this bad behavior still affects their former spouse and children.

This is common knowledge. Most people know either a friend or family member who is addicted to drugs or alcohol, so they are familiar with the devastation that addiction causes.

In marriage, it isn't possible for love to flourish if someone is addicted to alcohol or drugs. The couple can pretend for a while that everything is okay, but as long as the person is using, the marriage is on a crash course with disaster. There may be times when all seems to be normal, even good. But, in alcohol and drug addiction, the symptoms always worsen. Even if a person stops for a while, when he goes back he will quickly return to the former level of usage, then surpass it, just as if he had never stopped. This isn't deliberate. It's the way addiction works.

Behavior also worsens over time. Addicts often have affairs and otherwise act irresponsibly. Some are able to maintain jobs and even playact well enough to make extended family members and friends think they are functioning normally. Spouses know better, though. Over time they see firsthand that both the addiction and the behaviors are getting worse.

It takes awhile to wake up to the fact that a spouse is addicted. Initially, the wife of an addict will rationalize excessive alcohol or drug use. She may blame it on stress or pass it off as recreational use. When bad and irresponsible behaviors first appear, the addict quickly apologizes for them and is forgiven. Following unusually bad behavior, he often goes into a period of acting his very best.

This process drives the spouse nuts. Just when she decides she can't take anymore, the addict cleans up his act. During this time a state of euphoria can exist in the marriage. Everything goes so well that all the bad and irresponsible behaviors are swept under the rug. The partners, in essence, kiss and make up. The spouse is enormously relieved and thankful all the problems have gone away.

However, at some point the addict goes back to drinking or taking drugs. This may be hours, days, weeks, or even months later. Each time he does, the usage and behavior get worse. When these reach an intolerable level for the spouse, usage will again stop or lessen to the point that behavior can return to acceptable levels again. Then the cycle starts over. Eventually the addict will lapse into long periods of excessive use and deplorable behavior he cannot control.

Meanwhile, the spouse spends more and more energy trying to fix him and all the problems he causes. When she can no longer deny the problems or fix them, the marriage crumbles. If it doesn't end legally, it ends emotionally.

The only way out of this predictable scenario is for the addict to get some help. Rarely can a person beat an addiction on his own. Left to his own devices, the addict will go right back to drinking or taking drugs.

Even so, most addicts resist getting help. Addictions get such a grip on a person that they cause him to say and do anything to ensure a continual supply of the alcohol or drugs. He will make excuses or promise to get help, but will not follow through.

It's only when the addict's life falls apart that he has a chance of accepting help. Most spouses unwittingly thwart this from happening by assuming the addict's responsibilities and keeping him from bearing the consequences of his actions. Her intention is good. She's trying to get her spouse to stop using and to straighten out his life. The periods of no use and exemplary behavior perpetuate her hope that eventually things will be okay. In the meantime, she keeps fixing problems and doing whatever is necessary to keep the family afloat.

The best chance for the addict to get help comes when his spouse no longer covers up the problems. Then either she or his boss finally issues an ultimatum for him to quit and get help. Some alcoholics and drug addicts will do just that. Others are so in the grip of their addiction that they continue to use and deny help despite knowing they will lose their family or job.

If the addict does have a chance at getting help, it will probably come when the family or workplace intervenes. The most effective interventions result from the joint efforts of the family and the workplace. In such cases, the addict is confronted and offered help.

Interventions are best planned, prepared, and coordinated by professionals. Usually, by the time the family or workplace is ready to intervene, the addict is a danger to himself or other people. He may be driving while under the influence and the chemicals he is ingesting may be taking a toll on him physically. Other behaviors may also be endangering him or others.

If he can find any possible way out of the intervention, he will. That's why interventions are best left up to professionals experienced and skilled at helping alcoholics and drug addicts. Supported by ultimatums from the workplace and family members, professionals have a good chance of getting the addict to accept help.

If your spouse has a problem with alcohol or drugs, you will need to get some help. Don't wait until your partner is willing to agree to it. By that time it may be too late to save either your spouse or the marriage.

Help, fortunately, is readily available. Call a minister. They make referrals all the time and will know places that are supported by both private and public funds. Or check the yellow pages of your telephone book. Under "Alcoholism," you will find numbers for treatment centers and Alcoholics Anonymous. Even if the problem is with drugs, these people will know how you can get the help you need.

The good news is that there's help available for you. One of the best support groups for spouses is Al-Anon, the sister group to Alcoholics Anonymous. Both are twelve-step programs and have the greatest record of success helping alcoholics and drug addicts and their families. These caring, knowledgeable people have been through, or are still experiencing, exactly what you are going through. It's a wonderful feeling to talk to people who can relate to you. They will also help you find other avenues of help.

You may also find help through employee assistance programs. Most large employers provide counseling and referral services that can be used by employees and their family members. They are commonly referred to as EAPs. The personnel department will know the number to call or you can look in the yellow pages under "Employee Assistance Programs." EAPs will know all of the community resources available.

Community mental health centers and hospitals can also assist you. Call either and ask to speak with someone who knows community resources for alcoholism or drug addiction. You will be put in touch with someone who can help you.

The easy part is finding help. The tough thing is to reach out and get it. It's tough because if you are married to an alcoholic or drug addict, you probably don't want to admit it. Getting help causes you to face the reality and severity of the problems. This is painful to do. However, the best chance of getting the addict help happens when his spouse gets help. Waiting for the addict to get help is to wait too long. By the time he does, the problems caused by his bad and irresponsible behavior may be unfixable. Like cancer, the earlier addiction is treated the better the chance of a successful resolution—and the better chance children will recover from addiction-related family problems.

Love Potion

If your spouse has a problem with alcohol or drugs, find an Al-Anon meeting. Go to the meeting and participate or just sit back and listen. (Hint: These meetings are confidential.) If you go, you may tell your spouse or not. If you decide to tell, be prepared for a negative or even derisive reaction. Regardless, the important thing is to get some help for yourself. When you do, you may find an unexpected benefit: It may also turn out to be the first step in getting help for your spouse.

As I want all of my love potions to be positive, let me end on this happy note. Millions of people get help every day for addictions. Millions are also in recovery from these problems and lead happy and productive lives. Many of them also go on to be happily married for a lifetime.

Here is a self-test that will help you assess the level of commitment in your marriage.

COMMITMENT AND DEDICATION ASSESSMENT TEST

Instructions: Score the following statements from one to ten depending on how true you think the statement is about yourself. One is the lowest score and ten the highest. Total your score at the bottom. For privacy, score your answers on another sheet of paper.

_____ 1. When I come across something that's going to affect me, I also consider how it will affect us as a couple.

_____ 2. When I view the long term, I see us married in our retirement years.

_____ 3. I often sacrifice my own wants and needs if it will benefit my marriage.

_____ 4. While I may fantasize about someone else, I am not seriously attracted to anyone but my spouse.

_____ 5. I have a strong desire to maintain my marriage despite the difficult times.

_____ 6. My marriage is one of the most important things in my life.

_____ 7. Rarely do I think about what it would be like to be married to someone else.

_____ 8. My relationship comes first.

_____ 9. My vision for the future includes my spouse.

_____ 10. I get joy out of making sacrifices for my mate.

_____ **Total**

The total possible points are one hundred. On average, couples that report their marriages are happy and stable score about eighty-three points. If your score is similar then you are also dedicated to staying in your marriage. If you scored below a sixty-four, then your level of commitment to your marriage is low. Whatever your score is, consider how your attitudes about commitment may affect the future of your marriage.

Love Potion #58

Plan a ceremony to reaffirm your marriage vows. It can be anything from a simple, private ceremony with just the two of you to a major event with guests and a party. In either case, go to the library or bookstore and ask for a book on planning weddings. In it you will get some great ideas on how to make your ceremony special and meaningful to you. (Hint: A second honeymoon after the ceremony would be nice as well. If you can't plan a major trip, plan a special evening in town.)

Additional copies of *HAPPILY MARRIED FOR LIFE*
and other Life Journey titles are available
wherever good books are sold.

If you have enjoyed this book,
or if it has had an impact on your life,
we would like to hear from you.

Please contact us at:

LIFE JOURNEY BOOKS
Cook Communications Ministries, Dept. 201
4050 Lee Vance View
Colorado Springs, CO 80918

Or visit our Web site: www.cookministries.com